# GEORGIA

Picture Research by Kathryn W. Kemp

Preferred Marketing
Tarzana, California

# GEORGIA

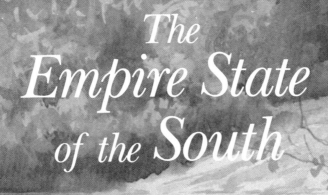

## The
## *Empire State*
## of the *South*

*Bradley R. Rice and Harvey H. Jackson*

Windsor Publications, Inc.—History Book Division

Vice President, Publishing: Hal Silverman

Editorial Director: Teri Davis Greenberg

Design Director: Alexander D'Anca

Corporate Biographies Director: Karen Story

Staff for *Georgia: Empire State of the South*

Editors: Pamela Schroeder, Lane A. Powell

Photo Editor: Susan L. Wells

Assistant Director, Corporate Biographies: Phyllis Gray

Editor, Corporate Biographies: Judith Hunter

Production Editor, Corporate Biographies: Una FitzSimons

Editorial Assistants: Didier Beauvoir, Thelma Fleischer, Michael Nugwynne, Kathy B. Peyser, Pat Pittman, Theresa Solis

Senior Proofreader: Susan J. Muhler

Layout Artist, Corporate Biographies: Mari Catherine Preimesberger

Design and Layout: Ellen Ifrah

Library of Congress Cataloging-in-Publication Data

Rice, Bradley Robert, 1948-

Georgia: empire state of the South / Bradley R. Rice and Harvey H. Jackson: picture research by Kathryn W. Kemp: Society. — 2nd ed.

p. cm.

Bibliography: p. 139

Includes index.

ISBN: 0-89781-480-0

1. Georgia—History. 2. Georgia—Description and travel—Views. 3. Georgia—Industries. I. Jackson, Harvey H. II. Georgia Historical Society. III. Title.

The Library of Congress has catalogued the Windsor Publications First Edition as follows:

F286.R53 1988

975.8—dc19

87-31688 CIP

Facing page: *Waterpower drove mills in early Georgia. This mill gave its name to Howell Mill Road, now a street in the elegant Buckhead area of Atlanta. Painting by Wilbur Kurtz. Courtesy, Franklin Garrett*

Previous page: *Enterprising property owners operated ferry services, like the one seen in this painting by Wilbur Kurtz, until railroads and bridges made the way more convenient. A century later, the site of this ferry was inside the city of Atlanta, and the road it served is now a city street which bears the name Montgomery Ferry Drive. Courtesy, Franklin Garrett*

Page six: *A rainbow of colorful flowers are a highlight of Georgia's spring days. Photo by Arni Katz*

# CONTENTS

# PREFACE

Of the original thirteen states, Georgia is the youngest and largest. More than a century passed from the founding of Virginia and Massachusetts to the time that James Oglethorpe and his fellow trustees established Georgia in 1733. Another century and many treaties passed before the Creek and Cherokee Indians were finally removed from the last of their Georgia homelands.

Even before the Civil War, proud boosters hoping for industrialization to complement the slave-based cotton culture had dubbed Georgia the "Empire State of the South." Yet Georgia, like the rest of the Confederacy, emerged from the Civil War in economic and social disarray. Well into the twentieth century Georgia remained a predominantly rural state lagging considerably behind national norms in objective measures of prosperity.

Glimmers of change appeared after the Second World War, and by the 1960s the claims of Georgia boosters began to ring true. If Georgia was becoming the Empire State, its imperial city was Atlanta. By the 1980s nearly half the state's population and over half of its economic activity was concentrated in metropolitan Atlanta. Only 150 years earlier the site of Atlanta had been nothing but a surveyor's stake marking the terminus of a projected state-owned railroad. As Georgia prepared to host the Democratic Party national convention in the summer of 1988, Atlanta was recognized as a major hub of the bustling Sunbelt.

We have endeavored to illuminate this process of historical change in words and pictures. Of course, we want our book to be popular, but it is not just a popular history. In a work of this length, authors must necessarily be selective, but we have not just selected from the rosy side of Georgia history. We believe that Georgia's considerable accomplishments can be best appreciated if one understands her formidable obstacles. But neither have we dwelt on the negative, for our goal is a balanced account. We hope that you will find that we have met our goal and that you will develop a new appreciation for Georgia's rich and colorful history.

As we attempted to draw on our scholarly backgrounds to produce a popular synthesis of Georgia history, it became clear to us that our biggest debt as professionals is to our fellow Georgia historians who have produced the hundreds of books and articles from which, throughout our careers, we have drawn in general and in the writing of this book in particular. We are also indebted to the Georgia Historical Society for having confidence in us as coauthors of the first edition of this book.

This second edition contains an epilogue that updates the story of our state's history to cover the exciting past seven years leading to the 1996 Olympic Games.

# 1

## A CLASH OF

## EMPIRES

*British aristocrats and merchants occasionally feted tribal dignitaries from the American colonies. These eighteenth-century Cherokees met the King and received their English clothing from him. Courtesy, University of Georgia Libraries Special Collections*

For James Oglethorpe and his band of colonists it must have been a strange sight. About an hour after they arrived at the bluff where Savannah would be built, they were greeted by the nearby Yamacraw Indians. Peter Gordon, one of the colony's first officials, described the scene:

*The King, Queen, and Chiefs and other Indians advanced and before them, walked one of their generalls, with his head adorned with white feathers, with ratles in his hands (something like our casternutts) to which he danced, observing just time, singing and throwing his body into a thousand different and antike postures. In this manner they advanced to pay their obedience to Mr. Oglethorpe.*

In the minds of the Georgia colonists, these Indians appeared to be children of the wilderness to whom the English would bring the benefits of civilization. What the colonists did not know, or at the time did not appreciate, was that the Yamacraw already provided visible testimony to the impact of European civilization on native Americans. Over the previous two hundred years, Southeastern Indians had dealt with the Spanish, French, and English. In the process

they underwent a transformation so radical that Georgia proved almost as new to them as it did to those who arrived on the *Anne*.

Few Indians lived in the territory Oglethorpe claimed. This had not been the case when the first Europeans landed. At that time the southeastern Indians, of which the Georgia tribes were part, boasted large numbers and possessed "the richest culture of any of the native people north of Mexico." Their ancient ancestors first came to the region as wandering hunters. Then, about 8000 B.C., Georgia tribes began to gather acorns and hickory nuts as a supplement to food obtained through hunting, fishing, and trapping.

These Indians' increasingly sedentary existence encouraged other innovations, and some of the earliest pottery in North America has been found at one of their villages on Stallings Island in the Savannah River near Augusta.

During the next 7,000 years, Southeastern Indians became increasingly efficient at hunting and gathering, and developed a more organized social system. They also developed a complex set of religious beliefs, which included a concern for the proper burial of the dead, as revealed by remains found tightly

bound and carefully placed in burial pits.

About 1000 B.C. a new Indian culture began to develop along the Mississippi and Ohio rivers, and in time it found its way to Georgia. While still hunting and gathering, the Indians now cultivated squash, gourds, and (later in the period) corn. They also developed better vegetable storage techniques, including the improvement, and more widespread use, of pottery.

Better food enabled the Indians to increase an already growing population. Larger, more permanent settlements emerged, serving as the foundation for an extensive trading network. Increasing population density also gave rise to a more complex social-political structure. Again, mortuary practices were refined to the point that these Indians produced the monumental earthworks that survive as their greatest accomplishment.

In Georgia, the earthworks are best represented at Kolomoki in the southwestern part of the state. At that site, a mound complex covering more than 300 acres is highlighted by a temple mound over 50 feet high, 325 feet long, and 200 feet wide. According to some estimates, two adjacent burial mounds required the labor of over 1,000 people —dramatic evidence of the size and organization of Indian towns. The state also boasts one of the most striking and mysterious animal effigy mounds: in central Georgia, near Eatonton, is Rock Eagle, a carefully constructed representation of a bird (eagle or buzzard) made from piled rocks. Measuring 120 by 102 feet, it appears most impressive when viewed from above. Because the Indian builders left no clues in the vicinity for researchers, Rock Eagle's purpose is still a mystery.

Between A.D. 700 and 900, a third culture began to spread from the Mississippi Valley into Georgia. It was invariably found in rich river valleys and along streams where soil proved best suited for more extensive agricultural use. Indians there raised an improved variety of corn, along with beans and squash. The sites also reveal an increased population, larger towns, and less emphasis on religion than during the earlier era. Large, steep-sided, flat-topped, pyramidal earth mounds often dominated these cities. As commercial and political centers, the settlements testified to the advanced social and economic development of Southeastern Indians.

At the Ocmulgee National Monument near Macon stands one of Georgia's most impressive archaeological sites. About A.D. 900 invaders dis-

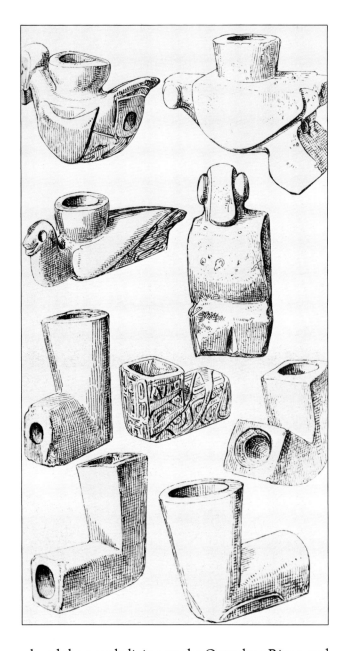

placed the people living on the Ocmulgee River, and over the following decades they built a town with mounds and unique earth lodges. Efficiently cultivating the river bottom, these people remained until around A.D. 1100, when for some unknown reason they disappeared. About 300 years later the area was reoccupied and a town (called Lamar by archaeologists) was established farther south. Its residents built a palisaded urban center with two temple mounds; cultivated the nearby bottom land; and consolidated control over the immediate area. In all probability descendants of these Indians greeted de Soto when he traveled through Georgia in 1540.

Among Georgia's Indian sites, none is more impressive than the mounds at Etowah in the northwest corner of the state. Here, along with the pottery and stone tools usually discovered at mound complexes, archaeologists found realistic white marble figures of

a man and a woman, both sitting cross-legged. Excavators also discovered large bowls, jars, wooden masks, monolithic axes, a polished stone disk with scalloped edges, and copper headdresses and plaques which depict men playing the role of falcons. Few sites can boast artifacts as impressive as those found at these mounds, and Etowah remains a relic of a culture far richer in symbolism and expression than that seen in most North American tribal monuments.

The first Europeans known to have visited Georgia's interior saw these Indians at the height of their cultural development. In March 1540 Hernando de Soto marched north from Florida, crossed the Flint River, and passed to the southwest of present-day Albany. Moving up the Flint, de Soto bridged the waters near where Dooley, Sumpter, and Macon counties come together. He entered a region called Toa, south of Montezuma, and stayed there briefly. From Toa the Spanish column headed toward the Ocmulgee River and the Kingdom of Ichisi; the main town was probably at the Lamar mound site east of Macon. There de Soto set up a cross and reported that the Indians worshiped it, though the explorer might have misinterpreted the native Americans' actions. Still traveling east, de Soto crossed the Oconee River,

moved through other kingdoms, and met other chiefs.

Hernando de Soto's ultimate goal was Cofitache-qui on the Cataba and Wateree rivers. To get there, however, he had to cross a "desert"—a vast stretch of unoccupied territory through which flowed the Savannah. De Soto's party finally marched through it and out of Georgia. A short time later they turned north, and after reaching the area near Asheville, North Carolina, they headed west and south, bringing them briefly back into Georgia's northwest corner and then into Alabama.

Not only did de Soto's band gain the distinction of being the first to see the Georgia Indians at the height of their development, they also proved to be the last. Even as the Spanish army entered the region, native Americans were falling victim to European diseases for which they had no resistance. By the time de Soto arrived, evidence of the impending biological disaster could be seen in towns "grown up in grass" and houses full of corpses, all from an epidemic that had struck the region two years earlier. Later observers mentioned conditions which indicate mortality rates of 50 percent or more.

The collective wisdom of generations vanished as

Right: *Spanish conquistador Hernando de Soto, the first European visitor to Georgia, came in search of gold. Two centuries would pass before the gold in Georgia's mountains was discovered. From Daly,* Adventures of Roger L'Estrange, 1896. *Courtesy, University of Georgia Libraries Special Collections*

Facing page: *Hernando de Soto, the first European to visit the area, followed this route through Georgia. Courtesy, University of Georgia Libraries Special Collections*

older tribesmen died and future leaders found themselves carrying out rituals without really knowing why. Mound centers were abandoned. When, decades later, Europeans asked about the purpose and creators of these monuments, nearby Indians could provide no clue. The mystery gave rise to all sorts of romantic stories of forgotten super races—even of European explorers who came, built, and departed.

More immediately, however, the epidemics forced survivors to reorganize. They joined with other tribes and in the process rearranged the social and political structure of the Southeast. It was a traumatic process which left the Georgia Indians ill-prepared to meet their upcoming challenge.

European interest in the Southeast was growing. In 1565 the Spanish founded St. Augustine to counter a French colonial threat. From there they moved up the coast to the island of Santa Catalina (St. Catherines), where in 1566 they met an Indian chief called Guale, whose name soon became synonymous with the whole area. The Indians pledged allegiance to Spain and the Christian religion; a garrison was put on San Pedro (Cumberland); and the Spanish colonization of the "golden isles" had begun.

Soon it was decided that missions should be established on the islands. Spanish Jesuits set to work, an effort which began discouragingly when the Indians clubbed to death one of the first missionaries shortly after he arrived. Other Jesuits followed, however, and they established a string of missions from St. Augustine to Port Royal. The purpose of these primitive outposts was to bring the Indians into the Spanish system, and establish a Spanish presence that would impede French and English efforts in the region.

Only the Santa Catalina mission has been found (the tabby ruins once believed to have been missions are actually old plantation outbuildings and sugar houses). From these remains we are learning much about the community's simple, indeed primitive, existence. Daub and waddle walls and palmetto frond roofs were the main type of construction; agriculture remained the primary occupation; and the chapel was the center of the village.

War with England in the 1580s made mission life all the more uncertain. Nevertheless, the conflict emphasized Guale's importance and caused the Spanish to take particular care for its defense.

In 1606 the Bishop of Cuba inspected Guale and reported that the region was secure and under the

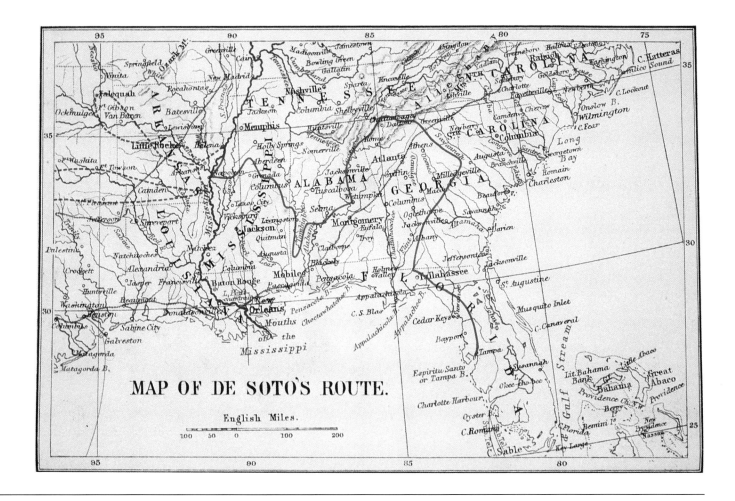

MAP OF DE SOTO'S ROUTE.

English Miles.

influence of His Catholic Majesty. This marked the beginning of what might be called the Golden Age of Spain in Georgia. Missions were built in the Apalachee region in the 1630s and the Spanish soon moved up the Chattahoochee as far as the falls. With the English settling Jamestown, Virginia, the year after the bishop's visit, however, Spain had a rival to challenge her control of the Southeast. Soon Virginia-based Indian traders began to move south, and Spanish protests were to no avail. Most important, these English traders dealt in Indian slaves, a venture which was to further transform southern tribal existence.

English businessmen proved quite different from Spanish missionaries in their approach to the natives. They provided arms to nearby friendly Indians and encouraged them to attack distant tribes, take captives, and sell them. This altered form of Indian warfare expanded conflicts throughout the region.

The founding of Charleston in 1670 accelerated the still-distant English threat to Spanish America's back door. Shortly thereafter, one of Carolina's earliest settlers, Henry Woodward, began to supply guns and ammunition to nearby Indians in return for slaves and pelts. Other Englishmen made similar agreements, and Charleston was on its way to becoming the center from which Britain challenged control over the Southeast.

With the coming of the Charleston traders, life for Indians in the region grew increasingly hazardous. One band's possession of European weapons threatened neighboring peoples, and soon the Indians were engaged in an arms race. Tribes united for their own protection, but they also sought to supply the English with slaves and deerskins in return for trade goods—particularly guns and rum. When the Indians made these new arrangements, settlements disappeared as quickly as they had during the devastating epidemics. It was not long before the traders turned their slave-catchers on Guale, where Indians trained in agriculture and accustomed to European systems of labor proved a handsome "catch." By the 1680s the island missions were losing population, and by decade's end the Spanish had abandoned Guale. A 100-year history seemed to fold overnight.

English exploitation completely disrupted and then remade the Indians' socioeconomic systems. By 1685 a small English trading post had been built near the Ocmulgee mounds at present-day Macon. Crowded around the stockade were the houses of the Ochese Creeks, who served the traders in a variety

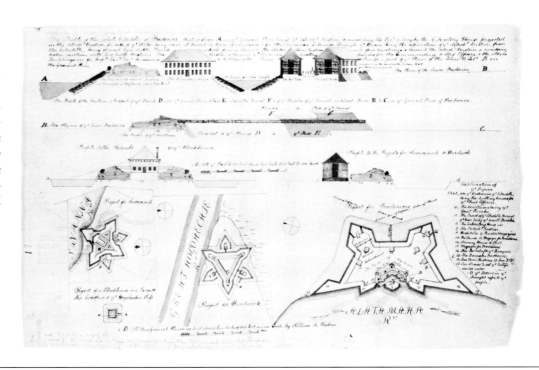

*Georgia served to block Spanish movement from Florida: this required fortified locations, such as Fort Frederica pictured here. Oglethorpe preferred Frederica to Savannah, and when the colony divided into two colonies, he made it the seat of the new county and spent most of his time in the colony there. Courtesy, University of Georgia Libraries Special Collections*

of ways. (Anthropologists note the similarity between the Ochese and the Ichisi—the Indians de Soto reported meeting in the same area.) These natives were the remnants of various tribes and towns that had combined to accommodate the English system. Before long the traders simply called them Creeks. In time that name was used by white men to identify all native Americans along the Chattahoochee and in the Coosa-Talapoosa River Valley, a practice which no doubt confused the Indians, who continued to think of themselves by their old tribal names. But what the Indians thought of themselves mattered less and less to the traders; white men accommodated the natives when necessary, but cheated and abused them when they could.

Georgia Indians were important in the expansionist ambitions of England, Spain, and France. In return for skins, information, and loyalty, these Europeans offered trade goods and protection. The Indians, skilled in backcountry diplomacy, played one interest off against the other, but an English victory in Queen Ann's War (1713) gave that nation the advantage. By the time the war ended, the only Indians left in the Georgia region were those who had reached an understanding with the Carolina traders.

The Charleston merchants remained far from fair in their dealings with the tribes, however. Indians were regularly cheated, insulted, and sometimes physically abused. As the lists of "crimes" grew, so did the Indians' anger. Most affected were those natives residing near white settlements, particularly the Yamasee tribe. The Yamasee lived near Port Royal, where they developed both a dependency and an increasing displeasure with their white neighbors. The traders' exploitation of these conditions severely tried the Indians' tolerance as the once proud people stood humiliated beyond endurance. Finally, in the spring of 1715, the Yamasee rose up and began killing any whites they could find. Panic seized the frontier as other outlying tribes joined the Yamasee, and settlers began fleeing their homes for the safety of Charleston.

For a moment it seemed that the Yamasee might win, but the same dependence which led to the conflict turned the tables against them. As ammunition ran out and guns needed repair, the Yamasee and their allies were forced to suspend critical operations; meanwhile, the Carolinians mounted a counteroffensive. The result was disastrous for the tribes; many dwindled to the point of extinction. Losses on the

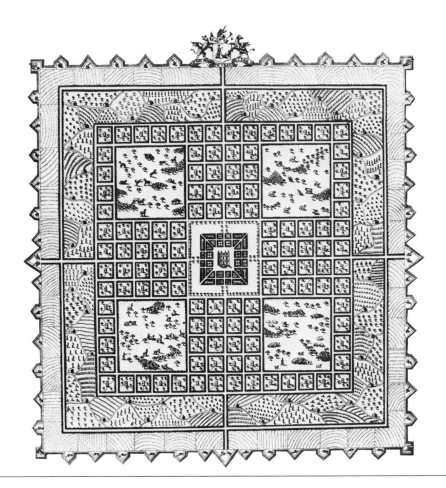

white side were also high (over 400 died, totaling about 6 percent of the colony's population). The Yamasee ceased to be an effective unit, but the disruption extended far beyond the Carolina tribes. The trading post on the Ocmulgee was deserted—its residents probably killed—and the Ochese Creeks fled west where they came under the influence of the French. Other Indians went south to the protection of the Spanish. But few natives remained in the region between the competing empires, the region that would shortly become Georgia. The land between the Chattahooche and the coast, between Carolina and Florida, stood open and inviting, and, depending upon the eventual occupant, potentially threatening.

Even before the Yamasee war created a vacuum below the Savannah River, English interests began to focus on more than the area's trading opportunities. The Scottish baronet Sir Robert Montgomery in 1717 proposed the creation of an elaborately organized colony called the Margravate of Azilia, both to guard the southern frontier and to produce exotic commodities for English markets. His plan received some verbal—but little financial—support, and the proposal quietly died.

More action was taken on a 1720 proposal by Carolinians John Barnwell and Joseph Boone. Seeking a British presence closer to the Spanish in Florida, these experienced frontiersmen recommended the construction of forts at the falls of the Savannah River, where important Indian trails converged, and at the mouth of the Altamaha. The latter, Fort King George, was soon built despite protests from Spain. Never popular with the soldiers who garrisoned it and of questionable defensive and diplomatic value, the post was abandoned in 1727. Nevertheless, its brief existence did signal England's renewed interest in the area. Carolina colonists, still reeling from the Yamasee uprising, hardly remained satisfied with one fort. When it was abandoned their concern grew. Therefore, the colony's governor, Robert Johnson, proposed the creation of townships along the frontier. These would be populated by citizen soldiers drawn from Ulster Scots and persecuted continental Protestants—an idea which later influenced Georgia settlement. Sentiment for English occupation of the so-called "debatable land" below Carolina was growing, and though the design of such an occupation needed to be determined, it was apparent that soon British authority would be extended farther south.

# 2

## GEORGIA IN THE

## BRITISH EMPIRE

*Englishmen who studied methods of producing silk hoped to make the precious fabric in early Georgia. Courtesy, University of Georgia Libraries Special Collections*

Above: *The seal of the Trustees of the colony of Georgia indicates that a cornucopia of profit was expected from investments. The two figures with water jars represent the Savannah and Altamaha rivers.* From White, Historical Collections of Georgia, 1854, *courtesy, University of Georgia Libraries Special Collections*

Left: *General James Edward Oglethorpe founded the colony of Georgia and personally organized early parties of settlers immigrating to America. His conception of Georgia as a buffer between the Carolinas and the Spanish, as well as a refuge for Britain's "worthy poor" reflected his philanthropic and military interests. This nineteenth-century engraving is courtesy of the University of Georgia Libraries Special Collections*

Historians still debate the reasons for Georgia's founding. Was the colony created to protect the southern flank of the Carolinas and to keep Spain and France from extending their influence over the area? Did military occupation simply provide a means of securing an economically valuable region for England's commercial empire? Or was Georgia a charity colony, a philanthropic endeavor carried out by selfless gentlemen who wanted nothing more than to give unfortunates a second chance? Not surprisingly, the answer to all three questions is yes. Of these motives, however, the third still captures the popular imagination. South of the Savannah River, the story goes, refugees from England's prisons—plus a sprinkling of persecuted Protestants—were offered a new life, one free from drunkenness, slavery, and unfair economic competition.

This emphasis on idealism and its role in shaping Georgia has perpetuated certain myths. For example, though historians have long known that Georgia's settlers were not recruited from English prisons and that only a handful were debtors, many people continue to cherish that romantic notion. Fortunately, this misconception provides an excellent place to begin a study of colonial Georgia; it also draws atten-

tion to the man with whom the colony and all its mythology is generally associated: James Edward Oglethorpe.

Even if he had not founded Georgia, soldier and statesman James Oglethorpe would have boasted a remarkable career. Indeed, his association with colonization came almost by accident. As a young member of Parliament, he was made chairman of a committee that looked into conditions in the country's jails. Shocked at what he found, Oglethorpe issued a scathing report condemning many of England's penal policies; as a result he became a national figure. The experience also planted in his mind the idea that many of these prisoners, some of whom were debtors, might be able to rehabilitate themselves if given a fresh start in a new land.

The notion of a new colony circulated, and soon it began to attract the attention of Englishmen who saw in it a way to promote their own particular causes or interests. This developed into the formation of a board of 21 prominent gentlemen—led by Oglethorpe—that included the likes of John Lord Viscount Percival, later the Earl of Egmont. In 1730 they requested a royal charter allowing them to settle the land between the Savannah and Altamaha rivers.

The charter was granted two years later, followed by the incorporation of "Trustees for Establishing the Colony of Georgia in America."

Georgia often has been pictured as a "planned" province. In certain critical ways, however, just the opposite was true. Despite the fact that South Carolinians knew the area well, the Trustees failed to utilize these settlers' store of information. Oglethorpe's promotional description of the region, made before he had ever set foot on Georgia soil, causes one to wonder if he had taken the trouble to consult anybody who had actually been there. "The air," he wrote, "is . . . always serene, pleasant and temperate, never subject to excessive Heat or Cold." Georgia's founding father wrote of soil "impregnated with such a fertile Mixture that they use no Manure," which would ". . . produce almost every Thing in wonderful Quantities with very little Culture." Fruit trees of all sorts were said to abound, and "from the Stone, [would] grow to be a bearing Tree in four or five Years Time." More amazing still, Oglethrope continued, "all Sorts of Corn yields an amazing Increase . . . tho' their Husbandry is so slight, that they can only be said to scratch the Earth and meerly to cover the Seed." Indeed, when Oglethorpe finished cataloging the wonders to be found, there was little reason to doubt that Georgia was just as Sir Robert Montgomery had earlier described it—"the Most delightful Country of the Universe."

But the Georgia Trustees' first priority was not to deal with the land as it actually was, but rather to make it what they wanted it to be. This presented some problems; each supporter wanted the colony to be different things for different reasons. Georgia became one of the most unique colonial experiments in the history of the British Empire.

The Trustees whose views initially carried the most weight were those wishing to make the colony a place where England's "worthy poor" could rehabilitate themselves by the sweat of their brow. These "charity" colonists would be allowed 50 acres of land, tracts considered more than sufficient to support a family in "fruitful" Georgia. The property would not be granted outright, however. The Trust planned to retain ownership, while allocating land to colonists who abided by established regulations. This would prevent unfit property managers from selling or mortgaging their American holdings and ending up in no better circumstances than when they left En-gland. To further guarantee success, each colonist was required to grow a certain number of mulberry trees on his land to feed the silkworms which promised to make Georgia and Georgians rich. Finally, the Trustees outlawed slavery. If settlers came to America to rehabilitate themselves through their own labor, owning and working slaves defeated the purpose. South Carolina, with its "idle" planter elite, was the example to be avoided. Conversely, Georgia would establish itself as a colony of hardworking, virtuous, yeomen farmers.

Those who supported the new colony for economic reasons saw no contridiction between this definition of labor and the land allocation plan. They believed that Georgia would yield exotic plants and products for a nation presently forced to buy silk, wine, and fruit from other countries. Moreover, Oglethorpe argued that "England will grow Rich by sending her Poor Abroad" for they would cease to be a drain on the nation and instead become productive citizens of the empire. This was a financially attractive and politically popular argument.

For many supporters, especially in the government, military considerations proved most important, and defense fit neatly into the overall design. Because Georgia was to be settled in small, contiguous tracts, each with an adult male present (women could not receive grants or inherit land), each could respond quickly and defend other settlements when attacked. Furthermore some supporters appreciated the absence of slavery, realizing that slaves would present a danger within the colony just as surely as the French, Spanish, and Indians remained a danger without.

Thus, the elements of the "Georgia Plan" were complementary and alterations would appear to weaken the entire proposal. This approach would influence the Trustees' thinking in the years to come.

By the summer of 1732, the venture began to take shape. Potential colonists who would be sent at the Trustees' expense were interviewed (a process that weeded out most debtors or convicts), and money was raised for what briefly became one of England's most popular charities. Oglethorpe announced his plans to depart with the first shipload, and by fall everything appeared ready. On November 17 the *Anne* set sail with some 114 settlers, and the Georgia experiment was underway.

On January 13, 1733, the *Anne* arrived at Charles-

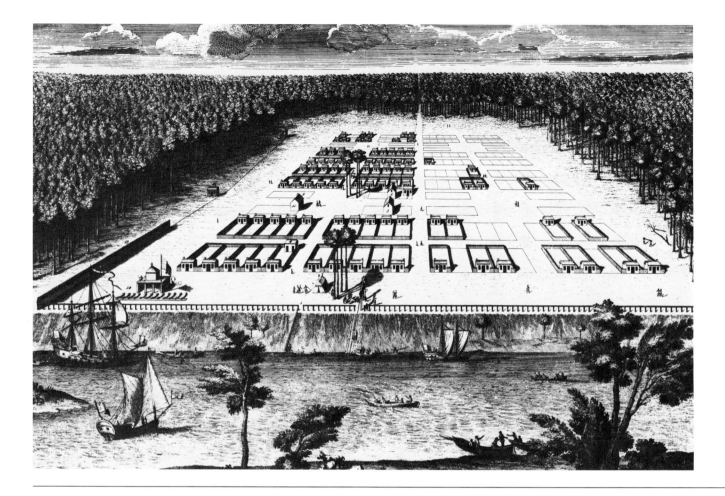

ton, and from there the colonists sailed to Beaufort where they disembarked for the first time. They waited there while Oglethorpe, joined by William Bull and other Carolinians, went ahead to select a site. The one chosen was on the Savannah River, "a healthy situation about ten miles from the sea . . . the river there forms a half moon, along the South side of which the banks are about 40 foot high and upon the top [was] a flat which they call a bluff." James Oglethorpe would lay out the town of Savannah on that spot.

Soon after arriving, Oglethorpe met Tomochichi and his Yamacraw Indians, who lived close to the nearby trading post of John Musgrove and his Indian wife, Mary (who served as Oglethorpe's advisor and translator).

Indeed, the Yamacraw were products of the transformation that tribes had undergone for nearly two centuries. They were "traders' Indians" who remained middlemen in a variety of capacities. The more English in the area, the more valuable their services—no wonder Tomochichi and his people greeted the Georgians with open arms!

Oglethorpe went back to Beaufort, collected the colonists, and returned to Yamacraw Bluff. The party disembarked on February 12, 1733. After spending the night in tents, they built a crane to unload the ship and began clearing the land for their village and farms. Oglethorpe "marked out the town and common." In less than two weeks the first houses were being built.

Although the colonists were expected to earn their keep by tilling the soil and defending the province if the need arose, only two of the 68 males claimed farming experience; none were soldiers. In the words of one observer, most proved to be "decayed tradesmen and supernumary workmen." They came with their families, and the majority hoped to build plantations. They looked to James Oglethorpe to guide them. Although Trustees were prohibited from holding colonial office, Oglethorpe, the only member of the board to visit Georgia, became the unofficial governor. The people called him "Father," and the local officers appointed to keep the peace and administer the rules sought his advice and example.

As the weather warmed, colonists began to suffer from "burning fevers . . . [and] bloody fluxes attended by convulsions and other terrible symptoms." Since the settlement's doctor, William Cox, had died earlier, there was no one to ease this suffering. Oglethorpe blamed it all on rum. The spirit was not yet officially prohibited and proved readily available to colonists

Left: *This eighteenth-century lithograph depicts Tomochichi, Chief of the Yamacraws, who gave General James Edward Oglethorpe rights to the land between the Savannah and Altamaha rivers. Tomochichi and a group of kinsmen returned to England with Oglethorpe, where they met King George II and Queen Caroline. Courtesy, University of Georgia Libraries Special Collections*

Facing page: *Peter Gordon produced this* View of Savannah *as it stood the 29th of March 1734 for the information of the Trustees of the colony. The neat pattern of residential lots and public squares remains visible in modern Savannah. Courtesy, University of Georgia Libraries Special Collections*

seeking some way to escape from the grinding, daily toil demanded of them. As conditions worsened a ship arrived with some 42 Jews, with Dr. Samuel Nunes among them. Jews were not among the "approved" colonists, but Georgia needed a doctor, and Georgia needed men, so the Jewish passengers were allowed to remain. Nunes' prescriptions of "cold baths, cooling drinks and other cooling applications" also proved beneficial; the crisis passed.

Early in 1734 Oglethorpe was ready to return home. He delayed his departure, however, when he learned of the impending arrival of the first shipload of Protestant refugees. Led by their ministers, Israel Christian Gronau and John Martin Boltzius, these natives of Salzburg, Germany, arrived in March and settled on a creek which ran into the Savannah River, near the passage of a principal Indian trail. There they built their village and named it Ebenezer. Oglethorpe—with Tomochichi, his wife, nephew, and five Yamacraw Indians—left for England the next month.

By this time James Oglethorpe had decided that Georgia's primary value to the empire was as a military outpost against the Spanish. On his return to Britain, he obtained parliamentary authority to establish a settlement farther south. In the fall of 1735, Oglethorpe set sail for Georgia with a flotilla of three ships and some 300 colonists. Most of the would-be settlers were bound for the southern frontier, where a band of Highland Scots recruited earlier had built the village of Darien at the mouth of the Altamaha River.

Oglethorpe set to work upon his arrival. Finding the Salzburgers unhappy with the land they had been allocated, he reluctantly permitted them to relocate in a better place. He also allowed the Germans traveling with him on this second voyage to settle with the Salzburgers—a considerable concession since he had planned for them to help defend the frontier. Then he took the other immigrants and sailed south, carefully putting the food and beer in the forward boat so the others would keep up or go without their rations. A few days later the colonists arrived on St. Simons Island; there they established the settlement of Frederica to guard the inland passage.

Not content to stop, Oglethorpe took Tomochichi, some Indians, and a party of Highlanders farther south "to see where his Majesty's Dominions and the Spaniards joyn." They planted forts on Cumberland Island and then went down the coast past Amelia Island to the mouth of the St. Johns River. He and his

John Wesley, the "Father of Methodism," served as an Anglican clergyman in colonial Georgia. His diary, which he wrote in his own code, is now in the Special Collections of Emory University's Woodruff Library in Atlanta. Courtesy, Robert W. Woodruff Library, Emory University

George Whitefield, the dynamic evangelist of the Great Awakening, visited Georgia on his many trips to America. In Savannah he founded the Bethesda Orphanage. Courtesy, University of Georgia Libraries Special Collections

band subsequently returned to Frederica, and in the months that followed established forts as far south as they had traveled. Spain, of course, protested, and the English withdrew from their southernmost post, but James Oglethrope had occupied the coast as far south as Cumberland Island for His Majesty George II.

Accomplishments notwithstanding, the colony was in trouble by the time Oglethorpe made his second visit to Georgia. One observer noted that "the poor who had been useless in England were inclined to be useless also in Georgia." The problem remained far more complex, however. Many settlers who tried hard to advance themselves and still failed blamed the Trustees' rules and regulations for their lack of progress.

Colonists' complaints were many, but their solution proved simple: they wanted larger grants, actual ownership of the land, and "the one thing needful"—Negro slaves. The Trustees felt that the rules should not be altered. If they were, large plantations would replace small farms and the people would live in fear of insurrection and invasion. The yeoman farmer for whom Georgia was created would be squeezed out: the "worthy poor" would be denied a chance to begin again and the frontier left exposed to invasion. Without regulations there would be no Georgia—or so the Trustees believed.

The center of protest was Savannah, which had gone into a decline when Oglethorpe made Frederica his headquarters. Leading the dissidents were colonists who had hoped to develop plantations along the Carolina model. Finding their land less productive than anticipated and unable to get the land they needed, they gravitated to Savannah, where Trustee supporters branded them the "malcontents."

By the time Oglethorpe returned to Georgia a third time, in the fall of 1738, divisions were deep. But James Olgethorpe—now the "General and Commander in Chief of the Forces of South Carolina and Georgia," with over 600 regular troops at his disposal—had other things on his mind. He quickly went south to fortify Frederica, an action which seemingly confirmed that Savannah and its dissidents would continue to be neglected and ignored. Pushed to the wall, the malcontents struck back.

In December 1738 some 117 freeholders from the Savannah area signed a petition calling for slaves and land ownership. Trustee supporters denounced the petitioners, and an outraged and worried General Oglethorpe sought aid to counter the critics. This came in the form of antislavery petitions signed by both Darien Scots and the Salzburgers. Malcontents claimed this support was "bought" by Oglethorpe and his allies; certain evidence suggests that indeed it was, but the tactic worked. With the favorable petitions in hand, the Trustees convinced friends in England that the protestors did not represent the majority of colonists. While settlers tried to make the best of an increasingly bad situation, leading critics of the Georgia Plan left for South Carolina where they formed a vocal expatriate band.

In the fall of 1739 England and Spain went to war, a course of action James Oglethorpe approved. The war focused world attention on the Georgia-Florida frontier. Along that perimeter Darien, Frederica, and Oglethorpe's other, smaller outposts prepared for the struggle, and the general organized his forces for a spring offensive against the Spanish in Florida. South Carolinians rallied as well, and the expedition became a joint one under Olgethorpe's command. But what began with such promise quickly became a disaster. Though the colonial forces got as far as St. Augustine, a Spanish surprise attack on June 15, 1740, broke the spirit of the invading army. By the end of the summer, troops were straggling back to complain of the expedition's poor organization and the "General's usage of them." Hopes for a quick victory dashed, a dispirited James Oglethorpe returned to St. Simons to consolidate his position.

The Spanish then began plotting an invasion of their own; by the spring of 1742 they were ready. In June Spanish troops landed on the southern end of St. Simons. Aware of the invaders' movements and superior numbers, Oglethorpe waited for a chance to strike. On the seventh of July the Georgia army of rangers and highlanders caught the enemy off guard. The resulting series of clashes, known collectively as the Battle of Bloody Marsh, saw some 200 of the invaders killed or captured, with the rest forced into retreat. The Spanish soon fled the island; Georgia and the southern frontier was safe.

Bloody Marsh marked the beginning of the end of Georgia's dependence on the military and of England's dependence on the province as a barrier against the Spanish. General Oglethorpe departed from Georgia the next year, never to return, leaving William Stephens, the Trustees' secretary, to oversee colonial affairs. With the military a less important aspect of everyday life, colonists shifted their attention to civil-

ian concerns. The issues which gave rise to the malcontents surfaced again. Demands for alterations in the rules, especially regarding slaves, were now heard outside of Savannah, where an economy once supported by garrisoned troops disintegrated into depression. Meanwhile, Parliament appeared reluctant to commit money to a colony which could no longer justify defense as a primary reason for continued subsidies. Moreover, the fire of reform was dying among the Trustees, and in its dim glow Georgians tried to find their way to a prosperity similar to that enjoyed by their northern neighbors.

Thus, in the decade after Bloody Marsh, the once-proud Georgia plan totally unraveled. Restrictions on rum, land, and crops were repealed or ignored; outlying settlements lay deserted; and Savannah emerged as the colony's capital in more than name. Peace with Spain was officially declared in 1748 and two years later slavery, "that one thing needful," came into practice. The malcontents had won; Georgia looked more like South Carolina every day. Rice was being grown in the swamps by black Georgians, whose labor would make many of their masters rich. Savannah began to appear as a small replica of Charleston, but the Georgia city's mercantile houses soon shipped their goods directly to England. Immigrants from Carolina and the West Indies came with their slaves, received large land grants, and all became Georgians.

The colony's political structure saw other changes. Under the original charter, the Trustees were to control the province only twenty years, at which time Georgia would revert back to the crown. However, a year before the expiration date, the Trustees confronted Parliament's reluctance to provide funds by surrendering their authority over the colony. In the ways that mattered most, the Trustees had already lost their control. With the original Georgia Plan largely swept aside, former malcontents were essentially running the colony; their masters in London proved little more than ciphers.

Thus, the colony passed into royal hands, and Georgians proudly advanced to a status equal to that of other provinces in the British empire. With this change in government came Royal Governor John Reynolds, who arrived amid cheers in October 1754. A new day seemed to arrive for Georgia. Her citizens had held the line against the Spanish; had successfully occupied the "debatable land"; and had provided a refuge for at least some needy arrivals. Nearly 6,500 col-

onists now proceeded to get on with the process of creating plantations from farms, and cities from towns and villages. Yet, the future appeared not as bright for some. In 1754 about 1,800 Georgians were slaves. For their masters at least, the bondsmen symbolized how far white colonists had come in their quest to match the accomplishments of other southern colonies. But slaves also served to remind those who cared just how far Georgia had strayed from her roots.

Captain John Reynolds, a navy man, arrived in Georgia amidst these sentiments. His purpose was to establish the new government and administer England's poorest mainland province for the good of its citizens and the empire. After the cheering stopped, a small band of influential, ambitious colonists viewed Reynolds' arrival as the next step in their ascendency to a position not unlike that of the merchant-planter princes of Charleston. As Georgia's elite, they remained determined to enhance and preserve their position. As members of the governor's council and the Commons House of Assembly, they constituted a small, interconnected ruling class, more provincial than counterparts in older colonies, but still the top of the Georgia heap.

Their center of operation was Savannah, further evidence of a malcontent victory. Though rural areas still held the bulk of the colony's population, Savannah and its environs boasted most of the representatives in the assembly and most of the members of the council. It would seem, therefore, that if Governor Reynolds expected to succeed, he would have to court these men. The governor, however, soon became entangled in a controversy which left him accused of creating and promoting his own faction in the assembly; favoring certain people over those more qualified to help him govern the province; and attempting to assume power not granted him by his office. Soon leading colonists were demanding Reynolds' recall. The London Board of Trade requested that the governor come to England for an investigation of the charges. When it was all done, the captain returned to the navy.

Reynolds was replaced by Lieutenant Governor Henry Ellis, who arrived in February 1757. Thirty-six years old, well-to-do, and a fellow of the Royal Society with a reputation as a scientist, Ellis seemed less suited for the duties of administration than had Reynolds. In the end, however, he proved far more qualified. Relying heavily on the advice of the governor of South Carolina—and therefore receiving directions that fa-

*This 1834 engraving honoring the centennial of James Edward Ogle-thorpe's agreement with Tomochichi and the Yamacraws was based on several familiar portraits. Oglethorpe gestures toward the seated* *Chief Tomochichi and his nephew. Mary Musgrove, the translator, stands between the two men. Courtesy, University of Georgia Librar-ies Special Collections*

vored Georgia's rising planter elite—Ellis healed most of the colony's divisions; put Reynolds' former critics in positions of trust and authority; and set the colony on a course parallel to, though decidedly behind, that of Carolina. It proved to be an approach to politics that ambitious Georgians could and did support.

Under Ellis the province grew and prospered. The population, just over 6,000 when he arrived, jumped to nearly 10,000 by the time he departed in 1760. Among the new colonists were a rapidly expanding group of black Georgians—slaves whose numbers increased from under 2,000 in 1754 to over 3,600 six years later. The colony's socioeconomic system reflected this change. Although most newly arrived whites settled in the backcountry, the majority of slaves were taken to the coast, where they cleared, drained, and diked the swamps to create rice fields, ultimately tending the staple that made their masters rich and powerful.

As the colony's planter elite grew wealthier, the merchants who carried their goods also prospered. Savannah was still a small, poor port when Ellis came to office. Only 52 ships cleared in 1755, but in 1772 over 150 vessels departed and another 56 left from Sunbury, a port which did not exist when the first figures were compiled. Certainly not a record to rival Charleston's, but for a colony so small it nevertheless represented a significant concentration of economic power in the hands of a few people. Henry Ellis catered to these men, and with their help he enjoyed a relatively trouble-free administration. Able to pursue his interests in natural history and science, he frequently walked about Savannah with a thermometer hanging from his umbrella, an experiment which convinced him that citizens of that city breathed the hottest air on earth. A bit of an eccentric (something Georgians have always enjoyed in their politicians) Ellis was truly liked, and when he stepped down in 1760 his departure was regretted.

Ellis' replacement was James Wright. Formerly South Carolina's attorney general and agent in London, he knew well the ambitions of Georgians trying to build a plantation system. Wright also realized that if a governor was to succeed, he had to cultivate public favor. Therefore, Wright's administration set out to advance the interests of those merchants and planters who had consolidated power under Ellis. What he did not realize was that there were other colonists ready to challenge these elites. James Wright had inherited a volatile situation.

# 3

# REVOLUTION AND
# REORGANIZATION

*After Lachlan McIntosh insulted Button Gwinnett, the two men fought a duel. Both men suffered wounds, but Gwinnett died three days later. McIntosh was acquitted of a murder charge and resumed his service in the Revolutionary Army. Courtesy, University of Georgia Libraries Special Collections*

One of the original settlers of Georgia, Noble Wimberly Jones actively supported the Revolution, participating in a 1775 raid on a Savannah powder magazine. After a brief, sometimes violent experience in Georgia state politics, he retired from public life to practice medicine until his death in 1805. Courtesy, University of Georgia Libraries Special Collections

James Habersham came to America in 1737 with the preacher George Whitefield. Habersham directed the Bethesda Orphanage and school in Savannah, and became a leading merchant, an important rice planter, and influential in the development of Georgia's colonial economy. Courtesy, University of Georgia Libraries Special Collections

James Wright seemed the ideal governor for Georgia. He understood the colony and its leaders; he wanted to promote trade, expand the plantation economy, and open more land to western settlers. He was willing, indeed anxious, for colonists to play a major role in governing themselves—provided they acted within the rules that made them subjects of the British crown. James Wright was the king's good servant, but he expected to be Georgia's as well.

In the decade and a half that followed Wright's arrival at Savannah in 1760, the colony grew and prospered. Its population increased from about 10,000 to some 40,000, nearly half of whom were black; with rice the major cash crop, export value grew to over £120,000 a year; new land was opened in the west, and that region soon contained the majority of the colony's white citizens. Georgia came to look more and more like South Carolina, just as the malcontents had wished. Indeed, many of the Trustees' former critics became prosperous planters and ranking officials in the government. They were the sort of people who welcomed Wright and who would be his chief supporters in the years to come.

Yet, in 1775 Sir James Wright was forced to flee the colony when the people he sought to serve joined the American Revolution. Just how many Georgians really wanted independence from England and why they chose that route is still debated today. The confusion reflects the chaotic nature of the era, for Georgia's revolutionaries ("Whigs") did not agree on their reason for rebellion or on what they wished to accomplish. Simplified, the Whigs consisted of three elements: (1) a coalition of rising planters, merchants, and politicians from or linked to the Savannah area, with a power base in the colonial assembly; (2) members of the backcountry planter-farmer-cracker class, who by the time of the revolution represented the majority of white Georgians; (3) a small but significant cadre of Puritan settlers from St. John's parish located midway between Savannah and Darien. At different times and for different reasons, these groups either supported or opposed Governor Wright's efforts to enforce British policies. In the end, however, they finally united against him. How that union developed is the story of Georgia's road to revolution.

It all had begun so well for Wright. England's victory in the French and Indian War (1763) gave Great Britain all of North America east of the Mississippi River. Spain was gone from Florida;

the French no longer controlled the west; and the Indians, unable to play one European force off against the other, readily negotiated with the victors. Secure for the first time in their colony's brief existence, Georgians prepared to enjoy their benefits as British subjects.

Meanwhile, the London government instituted colonial policies designed for more efficient and economical administration of the newly-won territories. These included regulations for the orderly settlement of the west, plus taxes to pay general operating expenses and ease the burden on a treasury heavily encumbered by war debts. The Proclamation of 1763, limiting expansion west of the Appalachians, set about to accomplish the first objective. Though it may have caused problems in other colonies, it actually expanded Georgia's southern boundary to the St. Mary's River. A treaty signed with the Creeks at Augusta in 1763 opened more land to settlement and further enhanced the governor's popularity.

Immigration into Georgia increased as colonists from the north (especially Virginia) headed south to seek land. They settled in the backcountry and became the foundation for that region's yeoman farmer class—and for the group known as "crackers." Though the origin of the name "cracker" is debatable (some claim it came from cracking corn, others from cracking a whip when driving stock to market), the characteristics which distinguished these people remain well known. Described variously as "persons who have no settled habitation and live by hunting and plundering the industrious Settlers," and as "a set of Vagabonds often as bad or worse than the Indians themselves," they were regarded with suspicion by red man and white man alike. Crackers also returned the sentiment, for if anything bound them together, it was their general unwillingness to abide by regulations which they felt were not in their interest; additionally, they shared a universal fear and hatred of the native Americans who occupied the land they wanted. One Indian chief may have said it best when he told officials, "these Virginians are a very bad people. They pay no regard to your laws."

Yet most Georgians were law-abiding citizens of the empire. The first of England's new taxes, the Sugar Act of 1764, produced hardly a ripple south of the Savannah. A year later the Stamp Act was protested, and the Sons of Liberty ("Sons of Licentiousness," Wright called them) made their appearance, but the governor enforced the law and Georgia became the only colony of the 13 in which stamps were sold. At this point, however, a small, but increasingly effective opposition party began to form; Wright found himself challenged by a new group of malcontents who proved just as determined to alter the system as their predecessors had been.

Wright's critics were led by an influential group of young men, mostly from or associated with Savannah. Their primary objective was to get the governor to share power with the legislature, on which many of them sat. Part of the establishment and hardly revolutionaries, they only wished a redistribution of authority to their advantage. Two of Wright's allies, Noble Jones and James Habersham, emphasized this point to the governor. Both had sons in the opposition movement. Although this half-hearted sentiment explained why Georgian protests seemed so subdued when compared to those of her sister colonies, other reasons existed. Georgians generally remained happy. Merchants and planters enjoyed an expanding economy, and in the backcountry the Indians were calm and land was available. This sort of situation hardly encouraged revolutionaries.

Between 1765 and 1774 Georgia's "Liberty Party" tried to gather support for its cause. Its strategy was simple. Wright would be challenged on a number of fronts and made to support unpopular policies (enforcing British taxes, interfering with the assembly's choice of a speaker, disallowing legal protests, etc.). The governor's opponents then might be able to show that the administration was out of touch with the people. Furthermore, Liberty party adherents could suggest broader public representation.

Wright's supporters responded that the dissidents did not champion the cause of the colonists, but only encouraged individuals to advance their own concerns, a charge which rang true to many. Interest and ideology had combined on both sides, and by 1774 they were impossible to separate.

It is unlikely that the Savannah-based "Liberty Boys" ever could have led Georgia to a revolution. Their numbers remained too small and their concerns too narrow. Wright seemed well in control of the situation as Georgia moved into the 1770s. However, in 1774-1775 two other factions joined the dissidents. Georgia's Whig movement took shape, ultimately dooming Wright. The coalition formed in 1774 when the Savannah faction called for a meeting

*A Connecticut Puritan educated at Yale, Lyman Hall was a physician and planter in Carolina and Georgia. After the British burned his plantation and accused him of treason, he and his family lived out the war as refugees, probably in Connecticut. He later returned to Georgia and served as governor, seeking to organize the state's finances and improve relations with the Indians. Courtesy, University of Georgia Libraries Special Collections*

*Button Gwinnett failed when he attempted to run a plantation, but was more successful in Revolutionary War politics. As Georgia's representative to the First Continental Congress, he signed the Declaration of Independence. Disputes with the McIntosh brothers in Georgia led to a duel with Lachlan McIntosh, which resulted in Gwinnett's death. Courtesy, University of Georgia Libraries Special Collections*

to denounce Britain's "Intolerable Acts." At that gathering in August, a large delegation from St. John's parish appeared.

St. John's had been settled in the 1750s by a Puritan congregation that had migrated from South Carolina to Georgia. Retaining "a strong tincture of Republican or Oliverian principles," they came with money and slaves. The Puritans built the town of Midway (on the road from Savannah to Darien) and the port of Sunbury, which by the 1770s vied for trade with Savannah. But some of St. John's leaders were upset at not having political power to match their prosperity. They saw the gathering that August as a chance to play a more prominent role in colonial affairs, and they seized the moment.

As these two factions—Savannah and St. John's—competed for leadership of the Whig movement, backcountry Georgians seemed at best unconcerned and at worst opposed to what was taking place. The Royal government protected them from the Indians, and in 1773 Wright negotiated a treaty which gave settlers access to land above Augusta. The coastal protests frightened many westerners, for if England was angered, the frontier might be denied the aid on which it depended. Thus, as lowcountry Georgians

signed petitions denouncing the British government, backcountry residents signed counter petitions claiming that the Whig movement, led "chiefly [by] those whose property lies in or near Savannah," did not represent their views or maintain their suppport.

Then, late in 1774, Wright made a move which seemed wise at the time but ultimately undid him: he negotiated yet another Indian treaty. This agreement, however, favored Indian traders and raised the possibility that the native Americans would be frequently passing through settled areas. Westerners in general and crackers in particular were outraged at this insensitivity on the governor's part. They rapidly switched their allegiance from the king to the Whigs, thus solidifying Georgia's revolutionary coalition. A short time later the St. John and Savannah factions temporarily set aside their differences, and in the summer of 1775 Whigs met in the colony's first provincial congress.

Earlier divisions in the Whig movement had prevented Georgia from sending an official delegation to the First Continental Congress, the only rebelling colony to be absent. Disgusted at the Savannah faction's timidity, St. John's nevertheless sent Lyman Hall as their observer. Georgians did select delegates for the second congress, which met in the fall of 1775, but by that time Lexington, Concord, and Bunker Hill were history; even reluctant Whigs found it difficult not to take a stand. Though most Liberty party members south of the Savannah were not yet ready to declare independence, they were prepared to carry their protests further. Still, many refused to become affiliated with the Whigs, and as long as Governor Wright remained in the colony these people retained some measure of power.

Meanwhile, the protests turned nasty. The Sons of Liberty, acting with the approval of the Whig Council of Safety, moved against their opponents, and punishments such as tar and feathering brought some of the most difficult into line. They took control of the colony and its administration, leaving Wright as governor in name only.

As the Whigs silenced their enemies, they began quarreling among themselves. In January 1776 a coalition of St. John's and backcountry delegates, upset with Savannah's dominance of the movement, elected Button Gwinnett, a planter with a history of bad debts, to lead Georgia's continental troops. Savannah Whigs were outraged and might have walked out had a compromise not been reached giving Lachlan McIntosh of Darien the command (Gwinnett went to the Continental Congress where he later signed the Declaration of Independence). Fearing that if Gwinnett and his supporters carried the day Georgia would fall "into the hands of those whose ability or situation in Life [did] not entitle them" to govern, the conservative-minded Savannah Whigs also had real doubts about broader democracy. Their sentiments were bound to lead to trouble in a movement that needed popular support.

A short time later McIntosh's small "army" repulsed a British attempt to resupply at Savannah; Governor Wright fled the colony and Georgia became a Whig state. News of the Declaration of Independence—signed by Georgians Gwinnett, Hall, and George Walton—was cause for celebration that summer, but conditions on the frontier kept the new government from being overconfident. British raids from Florida proved the Whig forces' weakness. McIntosh was hard-pressed to provide protection. Meanwhile, Georgia leaders remained utterly confused over how to organize defenses. General Charles Lee, recently dispatched south by the Continental Congress, observed that he would "not be surpris'd

if they were to propose mounting a body of Mermaids on Alligators."

If things were not chaotic enough, in the fall of 1776 Button Gwinnett returned to reorganize his political forces and challenge the conservatives for control of the Whig movement. The ensuing political contest was to influence Georgia for years to come. Forging an alliance of lowcountry and backcountry radicals seeking more popular government, Gwinnett gained control of the legislature. He then helped write Georgia's constitution of 1777, one of the most democratic to result from the revolution. Not only did this document give more people the right to vote, it divided the state into counties and apportioned delegates so that Savannah's power was reduced and, if the state's expansion continued as it had begun, the west would be the political force of the future. Gwinnett did not live to see his ideas come to fruition. Personal differences between him and Lachlan McIntosh reached a boiling point in the spring of 1777. After an expedition against St. Augustine failed because the two men could not cooperate, McIntosh publicly called Gwinnett "A Scoundrell & lying Rascal." Gwinnett responded with a challenge, a duel was fought on May 16, and three days later the signer of the Declaration of Independence died of his wounds. Lachlan McIntosh soon left the state to join General George Washington at Valley Forge.

Through the winter and into the spring of 1777-1778 Georgians held their own against British/Loyalist raids on the frontier. Then, in the fall of 1778, the enemy launched a campaign against Georgia and the South. The British attacks were uncoordinated until December, when an invasion force appeared off Tybee Island, and what followed was a fiasco. Shown an unguarded path, British troops avoided Savannah's defenses; the city fell almost without a gunshot. Those who could fled into the backcountry, and the victors prepared, in the words of British Colonel Archibald Campbell, "to rend a Stripe and a Star from the Flag of Congress."

The British acted quickly to secure their prize; then they moved up the Savannah River and captured Augusta. With the Whig militia still active locally, however, the town remained too exposed, and the British abandoned it on February 14. That same day Whigs defeated a large Loyalist force at Kettle Creek in Wilkes County. This raised American spirits, but morale sunk again on March 3 when the British sur-

Below: *Elijah Clark, although an illiterate backwoodsman, successfully led Revolutionary partisan forces against the British. After the war, he campaigned against the Indians and the Spanish in Florida. Although Clark died a deeply indebted man, his memory is revered by Georgians. He became the symbol of the backcountry yeoman farmer. Courtesy, University of Georgia Libraries Special Collections*

Below: *In spite of his father's loyalty to the Crown, Joseph Habersham played an active role in the Revolution as a member of the Liberty Boys and later as an army colonel. In 1795, Washington named him postmaster general. In 1801 he resigned, returning to Georgia and his interests in banking and planting. Courtesy, University of Georgia Libraries Special Collections*

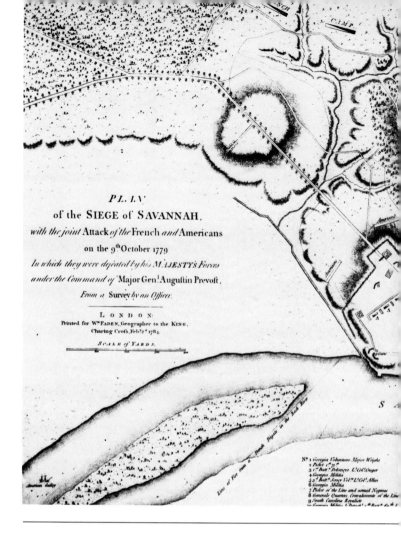

prised and defeated a patriot army at Briar Creek. Meanwhile, various Whig committees tried to "keep up a show of Government," but old divisions reappeared, and in 1779 Whigs seemed to fight each other as much as they fought the British. Differences were set aside briefly that fall when French forces arrived to join an attack on Savannah. Everything pointed to victory, but delays and poor execution doomed the project, and dispirited Whigs began arguing among themselves again. Soon Georgia was plunged into a round of fighting so devastating that it eclipsed all previous battles. The British took the offensive. In May 1780 Charleston fell, and in June royal forces captured Augusta. The Whig government all but disappeared and, as one historian observed, "it was every man for himself in Whig Georgia." A civil war broke out as former friends and neighbors fought each other. Violence and vendetta were the order of the day, and bands of partisans roamed the countryside. According to Henry Lee, Georgians on both sides "exceeded the Goths & Vandals in further[ing] their Schemes of plunder[,] murder & ininqu[i]ty." The legacy of bitterness left behind would not easily be forgotten.

But by 1781 Georgia's future began to seem more

Left: In 1779 a combined force of French and Americans failed to take Savannah from its British occupiers. Because of the lack of coordination between the two allies, the British held the city until 1782. This map, published in London, depicts a British account of the failed attack. Courtesy, University of Georgia Libraries Special Collections

Below: George Walton, a 26-year-old lawyer, was the youngest signer of the Declaration of Independence. Wounded and captured during the British assault on Savannah, he later served as governor of Georgia, delegate to the Continental Congress, and first chief justice of Georgia. This nineteenth-century engraving is courtesy of the University of Georgia Libraries Special Collections

hopeful. In April the Whig militia under Colonel Elijah Clark laid seige to Augusta and the town fell two months later. Slowly the British retreated toward Savannah. Georgia's government started to function once again, and by the beginning of the next year an assembly met in Augusta with every county represented. Though the victory remained elusive, the British apparently were losing their will to continue. Former Tories, hoping to exempt their estates from confiscation, swore allegiance to the new order, and the long, slow healing process commenced. Finally, on July 10-11, 1782, Savannah was evacuated. Those Georgians who could not accept an American government left, and the state was firmly in Whig hands.

From Florida, Georgia Loyalist Robert Baillie wrote his personal friend and political adversary Lachlan McIntosh about life in exile and how "this Cursed War has ruin'd us all." McIntosh partially agreed, for conditions in postwar Georgia lent skepticism to the accomplishments of victory. The economy remained shattered. Coastal rice plantations and frontier farms lay in ruins; slaves and stock were missing; commerce at Savannah halted. Sunbury and Darien were at a standstill; Indian trade was chaotic; and the state and its people lacked the capital to begin the long process of restoration.

The state's primary asset remained its land, which extended all the way to the Mississippi. Governor Lyman Hall pointed out the obvious: Georgia needed people. The state began dispensing liberal grants to army veterans, continued the colonial practice of granting land to family heads, and proposed to sell the remaining property at good prices and terms. Real estate profits would provide money for immediate needs, while taxes paid by new citizens offered a steady revenue source for the years to come. Given this view of the future, it is hardly surprising that the west was so important to postwar Georgians.

Thus began Georgia's efforts to extend her boundaries. The movement of the state capital clearly shows the direction leaders were looking. Savannah once again became the seat of government after the war, but soon the legislature also started meeting in Augusta. Recognition of the rising west became official in 1786, when the assembly—now dominated by what was once the backcountry—ordered that a new capital, Louisville, be built on the Ogeechee River, closer to the frontier. Not actually occupied until 1795, Louisville enjoyed a brief period of prosperity, but its main function as a center of land transaction seemed less essential as the frontier receded. Early in the next century the legislature created yet another capital, Milledgeville, even farther to the west.

But expansion was not as easy as creating capitals, for the Creek Indians and their talented leader, Alexander McGillivray, contested Georgia's claim to the land. Son of an Indian mother and white father and educated in Charleston, McGillivray knew what to expect from Georgians, and, with the Spanish back in Florida, he showed himself to be a master at playing one power off against the other. Georgians cared little for the rules of diplomacy or for the traditions of the Creeks. Believing a treaty with one Indian to be as good as a treaty with another, state officials negotiated land cessions with any chief willing to sign and announced that a clear title had been obtained.

McGillivray refused to accept these treaties, and when frontiersmen moved into the disputed territory, fighting broke out. Despite almost yearly negotiations between 1782 and 1787, tensions continued to rise, and the possibility of a general Indian war appeared very real.

Georgia lacked the resources to defeat the Creeks, but leaders realized that the Indians had to be removed from western lands if the state wished to relieve its financial burdens through real estate sales. Under the Articles of Confederation, the national government attempted to resolve this crisis, but Georgians wanted an arrangement which would give them the land on their own terms—something that federal negotiators refused to accept.

Georgia's Indian problems and the lack of support from the federal government partially explain why the state—later an opponent of strong centralized power—readily accepted the 1787 national constitution. Georgia needed help and hoped that a new government could provide it. The constitution arrived in October 1787, and a special convention was convened on December 28. Without opposition, the delegates formally ratified the Constitution of the

*Post-revolutionary Savannah boasted such civic improvements as this water tower. From White,* Historical Collections of Georgia, *1854, courtesy, University of Georgia Libraries Special Collections*

United States on January 2. Georgia electors also unanimously voted for George Washington to be the first president of the new republic in 1789, and the next year Washington convinced Alexander McGillivray to come to the nation's capital, New York. There the chief signed a treaty granting Georgia the land east of the Oconee River. Georgians denounced the treaty, however, because it recognized Creek claims to other territory. Thus began the states' rights debate that would soon become a staple of Georgia politics.

Neither Indians nor questionable claim to the territory between the Oconee and the Mississippi could deter Georgians from dreams of expansion and empire. This led to one of the most famous events in Georgia's early history: the Yazoo land fraud. For some time land companies had unsuccessfully tried to obtain control of the state's holdings. Finally, in 1794 a coalition of four Yazoo companies bribed enough assemblymen to get a bill through the legislature releasing between 35 and 50 million western acres for some $500,000.

The extent of the corruption soon became known, and legislators stood accused of selling Georgia's birthright. Georgia's U.S. Senator James Jack-

*Several folktales surround the adventures of frontierswoman Nancy Hart. In this cartoon, she has captured a group of surly Redcoats who had invaded her home seeking a free meal. The truthfulness of the Nancy Hart myths is unknown, but she was a real person who lived in Revolutionary Georgia. From White, Historical Collections of Georgia, 1854, courtesy, University of Georgia Libraries Special Collections*

son resigned his seat and returned to lead a movement to rescind the land sales. This resulted in the defeat of most of the legislators who sat in the infamous session. In the flush of victory the newly elected politicians repealed the act; then they gathered the Yazoo documents and, using a magnifying glass, set them ablaze "with fire brought down from heaven." For Georgians the repeal was a monumental victory; it also made James Jackson one of the state's most popular leaders.

Georgia was evolving rapidly as the eighteenth century drew to a close. New land opened up, and with grants available almost for the asking, the state's population increased. Speculation remained a problem, however, and smaller but equally demoralizing land frauds continued to be discovered. Rice production slowly rose to prewar levels, yet the future of that crop as the state's staple appeared doubtful since it could not be grown beyond the coast. Upcountry farmers cultivated corn, wheat, and some tobacco, and raised a variety of stock. Although most were only incidentially involved in commerce, this frontier subsistence soon began to change.

In 1793 at the Mulberry Grove plantation—which grateful Georgians had given to General Nathanael Greene— the family's tutor, Eli Whitney, invented the cotton gin. It marked the beginning of a revolution. As a result, the upland cotton, which would flourish on most of the western land, could be economically grown and processed. Soon plantations began to replace farms, and slave labor, once found primarily on the coast, expanded inland.

The prosperity Georgians had sought since the Trustee era seemed at hand. Augusta became a major commercial center, while Savannah began to undergo the economic boom that would make her one of the region's major cotton ports. Cooperation between east and west, coast and backcountry, seemed to herald a better age. Though political divisions existed, they were hardly as bitter as those which had divided the state earlier. The Georgia constitution of 1798 kept government in the hands of the elected assembly, but as the fledgling western counties developed it appeared clear where power would reside. And with three-fifths of the slaves counted for purposes of representation, the planter class established a principal role in governing. Indeed, optimism and hope loomed large for white Georgians. All was not well, but it was surely getting better.

# 4

# THE EMPIRE STATE

# OF THE OLD SOUTH

*Boston writer M.M. Ballou admired the town of Rome, Georgia, for its spacious layout and its "neat, pretty and unostentatious" buildings. He reported that this city of 3,000 residents shipped about 200,000 bales of cotton annually. Rome, a county seat, boasted a courthouse, three churches, schools for men and women, Odd Fellows and Masonic halls, covered bridges, and numerous commercial enterprises. This view of the city, which accompanied the 1856 story in Ballou's Pictorial, was made "from a drawing by Hill, reduced from a most elaborate delineation made for us by Mr. A. Grinevald on the spot." Courtesy, University of Georgia Libraries Special Collections*

*These gold miners are hard at work in the mountains of northern Georgia. From Blake and Jackson, Gold Placers . . . Dahlonega, 1859, courtesy, University of Georgia Libraries Special Collections*

As the nineteenth century dawned, Georgia was beginning to experience the growth that would make her the "Empire State of the Old South." Between 1790 and 1800 her population almost doubled, from 82,000 to 162,000, and most of the increase came from new settlement of the western land. The state's influence extended as well as her boundaries, keeping pressure on the Indians who remained Georgia's neighbors to the west. Despite the impressive expansion, some turn-of-the-century observers pointed out that though Georgia had "rapidly increased in population and riches . . . she cannot boast of equal rapidity in arts, sciences, and literature. With respect to these embellishments of civilized society, Georgia is still in the *Gothic Age*."

Most Georgians remained closer to the wilds of the "frontier than to the drawing rooms of a Tara." Ambitious Georgia farmers seemed "indolent and dissipated; not very scrupulous as to their moral character; fond of money to excess, but careless by which means it was obtained," according to one contemporary commentator. They also maintained a firm belief in their own abilities and in the democracy of hard work.

Frontier farmers wanted land, and their almost insatiable desire led the state to one of antebellum America's most remarkable examples of state economic and social engineering: the Georgia Land Lottery. The state distributed the rich central and southern Georgia cotton land in 202.5- and 490-acre lots, with winners paying only a small administrative fee. Every free white male citizen—plus widows, orphans, etc—got a draw. Over three-fourths of Georgia's public land was distributed in this manner, and many landless Georgians became property owners.

Unfortunately, the land lottery brought little money into the state's coffers. Furthermore, the legislature was reluctant to tax the new owners. Thus commenced a pattern and attitude characteristic of Georgia politics through the nineteenth and well into the twentieth century. "In the house of assembly," a critic observed, "a member who aims at popularity has only to oppose all public works and improvements that are likely to take the money out of the pockets of the people and he is sure to gain his end."

Certain circumstances necessitated collective action, however. The territorial push inland caused white settlers to once again come into conflict with their Indian neighbors. The Creek and Cherokee tribes had hoped to keep what remained of their land and sought accommodation with the whites. By the early nineteenth century though, it was obvious that most Georgians were unwilling to compromise. The former colonial backcountry now contained the bulk of the state's population. As this rich region filled up, covetous crackers began looking at the lands beyond the Ocmulgee River.

Shortly after 1810 the pressure on the Creeks and the Cherokees began. Both tribes had attempted to adopt white ways—farming, business, etc.—but many of the Creeks found little success or satisfaction in those occupations.

The Creeks soon came to view America's war with Britain in 1812 as an opportunity to secure their land. After its defeat at Horseshoe Bend, Alabama, the following year, however, the tribe was treated like a vanquished enemy rather than as a nation with which to negotiate. Though the Creeks vowed to hold their territory, the tide of white expansion proved too great, and in the years that followed their holdings were slowly and steadily ceded to the state. Finally, Chief William McIntosh signed the 1825 Treaty of Indian Springs, and Georgia Governor George M. Troup (who ironically was McIntosh's first cousin) announced that the state possessed all Creek territory within its borders. Angry tribesmen later murdered McIntosh, but their revenge hardly altered the final settlement: the land remained Georgia's.

The Cherokee proved another matter. Adopting the white man's ways to a greater degree than other Indians, they were generally regarded as the most "civilized" of the tribes. Most were small farmers, though some became slave-holding planters, and many accepted Christianity. With an alphabet developed by their remarkable tribesman, Sequoyah, they published their own newspaper, the *Cherokee Phoenix*. Cherokee leaders governed at their capital, New Echota, near present-day Calhoun. A constitution gave them most of the trappings of nationhood and attested to their skill as statesmen and politicians. Praised by the missionaries who lived among them and admired by observers outside the state, the Cherokees seemed to provide ample evidence that Indians could find a place in the United States.

But Georgians remained unimpressed. They wanted Cherokee land, and when the tribe resisted, the state applied new pressure in 1828 by extending its laws over the nation. This action was taken in part to guarantee that whites already on Indian territory would not be subject to tribal authority. Although the Cherokees initially ignored this intrusion, everything changed when gold was discovered there in 1829. Thousands of whites joined America's first "gold rush," and questions of jurisdiction became critical. The Indians ultimately sought protection in the federal courts, but it was Georgia's turn to ignore the orders of an external power. Finding a friend in President Andrew Jackson, who refused to enforce Supreme Court decisions favoring the Indians, Georgians convinced some tribal leaders that resistance was useless. In 1835 these chiefs signed the Treaty of New Echota and agreed to migrate in return for $5 million. The last of the Cherokee had been assembled and sent west on the "trail of tears" to Oklahoma by 1838. A few fled to the mountains where they remained to preserve the culture that was once so powerful in the Southeast.

Meanwhile, increased settlement led to economic prosperity. Most of the men who cleared Georgia's western land raised cotton. During the Revolution, cotton had been "planted only by the poorer class of people, just enough for their family consumption," but by the turn of the century it was the "never-ceasing topic" of conversation. Augusta became the upcountry's port city, with cotton warehouses lining the river. A visitor traveling up the Savannah River sought conversation with his fellow voyagers, but found that they "talked only of cotton, cotton, cotton." Bored, he "fled away from these worshippers of cotton."

In the popular mind, cotton meant plantations, which conjures up images of *Gone With The Wind*. Tara, Scarlet O'Hara, and Ashley Wilkes prospered in a polished and poised world where ideals of honor and chivalry dominated and where more men could read Latin than English. Interestingly, if Georgia ever boasted such an existence (and that is debatable), it was found mainly along the coast. There rice remained king and older families had established a more cultured way of life which stood in contrast to that of their counterparts on the cotton frontier. The estates of Thomas Spalding of Sapelo, James H. Couper of Hopeton, and Frances Henry McLeod of Wild Heron were often cited by visitors as pinnacles of the "southern way of life." Most Georgia planters and plantations failed to obtain anything even re-

Above: *Nineteenth-century Georgians drank or bathed in mineral springs to protect or restore health.* From White, Historical Collections of Georgia, 1854, courtesy, University of Georgia Libraries Special Collections

Right: *Modern Georgia potters still produce jars in the forms seen in this picture, titled "Plantation Well."* From Eickemeyer and Harris, Down South, 1900, courtesy, University of Georgia Libraries Special Collections

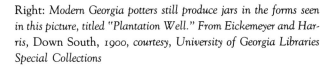

motely akin to that status, however.

One must not forget that Georgia was an evolving frontier society. To attain the "planter" status by the eve of the Civil War, Georgians (or their parents) had to have risen from frontier farmers. Indeed, one reason why the lower economic classes often voted for the more successful landowners was that they both frequently came from the same background. To go so far so quickly, Georgia planters displayed many of the economic traits usually ascribed to the more acquisitive, profit-oriented "Yankees," and if the South developed a more genteel way of life than the North, it did so in a way that most businessmen would recognize and appreciate.

Another reason why the small farmer sought the planter's leadership was that the latter controlled the South's "peculiar institution"—slavery. Three-fifths of Georgia's farmers claimed no slaves, and the majority of the slaveholders had fewer than six. In personal terms, therefore, most Georgians did not come in contact with blacks on a daily basis, but many of those who did worked side-by-side with their chattel. From the slaves' perspective the plantation was home. The majority of blacks dwelled in units of 20 or more people. Thus, they were able to establish and sustain relationships with each other, adding meaning to lives mostly consumed by labor.

This concentration of blacks on plantations placed an additional burden on the planter. Beside his responsibility for the bondsmen as laborers, he had to confine them to their quarters after working hours so they did not present a threat to the community. Whites felt the need to patrol because slaves frequently left their home plantations to visit friends and family nearby. The sense of a larger black community, however, ultimately helped ease the transition when freedom finally came. Music, folklore, religion, and art provided black Georgians a means of individual and community expression and gave modern Americans a unique, impressive heritage.

Slaves exerted their individuality in other ways, often simultaneously striking a blow at the system which oppressed them. Organized rebellion was rare and swiftly punished. Just before the Revolution a slave who led a brief uprising near Darien was captured, taken to Savannah, and burned alive in a public square. More often, however, lesser acts of resistance took place—chores not done, equipment broken, food or clothing purloined. Still, the best documented act of rebellion occurred when blacks "stole

themselves." Newspaper advertisements make it clear that runaway slaves were a major problem for both masters and for their nonslaveholding neighbors. For blacks, though, these escapes provided a taste of freedom and a chance to take their lives into their own hands. Georgia was too far from free territory to offer slaves much hope of permanent liberty, but that hardly seemed to matter. Freedom proved dear, and worth the risk.

In the meantime, Georgia continued to grow. Towns and communities which appeared like stepping stones for the expanding population charted western progress. In the fall-line cotton belt were the new state capital, Milledgeville (1806), and Athens, the seat of the state university. Other nearby towns reflected the state's patriotism and political leanings—Washington (1804), Jefferson (1805), Madison (1809), Monticello (1810), and Monroe (1821)—but more significantly, they provided market centers for the thriving cotton economy. Creek concessions were reflected in the founding of Macon (1823) on the Ocmulgee, and Fayetteville to the northwest that same year. The tribe's final departure paved the way for Thomaston in 1825 and for Columbus and La Grange three years later. Thomas-

ville (1831), Americus (1832), and Albany (1832) attested to the growth of the southern part of the state, while the gold rush and the Cherokee expulsion created Dahlonega (1833) and Rome (1834) in the northwest.

Like the people who settled them, these proved to be rough and tumble communities. Across the river from Columbus was a village where the "lowest stage of drunkenness and debauchery prevailed to such an extent that the settlement had acquired the nickname of Sodom." Though Georgians might take comfort that the town was in Alabama, careful inspection would have revealed a number of similar scenes east of the Chattahoochee. With the possible exception of Savannah, Georgia's antebellum communities were rural in orientation, democratic in social and political outlook, and crude in cultural attainments.

Yet, the rough edges soon began to smooth. In most communities a church, or churches, were the focus of a collective search for order and respectability, and during the first half of the nineteenth century a religious establishment might be the only organized social unit in a given area. Not every denomination was suited for the expanding backcountry, however. Episcopalians, Congregationalists, and Lutherans suf-

Right: *Georgia planters experimented with sugar cane in the warmest, southernmost regions of the state. The sugar crop never approached the profitability of cotton as a commercial undertaking because cold winters inhibited its growth. From Eickemeyer and Harris,* Down South, *1900, courtesy, University of Georgia Libraries Special Collections*

Facing page: *The kitchens on a plantation were separate buildings to minimize the risk of fire. Although the photograph "Solid Comfort" shows a simple stew pot, plantation cooks produced elaborate main dishes and baked goods in fireplaces such as this one. After the Civil War, the cast iron cookstove ended fireplace cuisine. From Eickemeyer and Harris,* Down South, *1900, courtesy, University of Georgia Libraries Special Collections*

fered to various degrees from their association with the coast. Reliance on centralized authority and requirements for an educated clergy further impeded their efforts to make inroads in less settled towns. Presbyterians had the burden of Calvinist theology, and the doctrine of predestination did not sit well with the democratic frontiersman. Interestingly, as farmers became planters the idea of an "elect" sometimes became more appealing, and as communities matured those who climbed to the top of society often chose Presbyterianism.

The most successful frontier churches, however, were Methodist and Baptist. Though the former retained its Episcopalian roots, circuit riders like Francis Asbury soon overcame these restrictions. Methodist clergy traveled from town to town, planting churches and entrusting lay leaders with the authority to act when no ordained minister was available. A fundamental emphasis on shared conversion and the equality of men before God further touched the hearts of frontiersmen. It also gave Methodists an advantage over their more formal, exclusive competition.

The Baptist church proved even more successful. Coming out of the Second Great Awakening of the early 1800s to challenge other denominations, they practiced congregational democracy and willingness to accept clergy on the basis of religious calling rather than formal training. Like the Methodists, Baptists gave their members a sense of community, of belonging, of mutual concern and caring. To know that friends and neighbors were looking out for each other seemed comforting in a region just establishing itself, where people lived as close to failure as to success and where life appeared uncertain at best.

Black Georgians also found comfort and a means of self expression in the religious surge of the antebellum period. Often present at revival meetings, they understandably welcomed the idea of equality in the sight of God. Though ministers and planters stressed slavery's Biblical foundations and the need to maintain the status quo, the liberating theology of the scriptures was not lost on black Georgians. Furthermore, Christianity offered them a degree of previously unknown or unappreciated control over their own lives. In most cases this spirit had to be obtained through the master's church and minister, but occasionally blacks themselves took charge. The First Colored Baptist Church, founded in Savannah in 1788, was one of a handful of congregations where

black Georgians could use their organizational skills to their own advantage. Though not always welcomed by whites, such experiences proved moving and meaningful for the few blacks who were able to participate.

While religion gave momentum to a richer black identity, cultural accomplishments even in the cities and towns of antebellum Georgia reflected the frontier influence. Outside Savannah it remained difficult to find what was generally considered "good society," and when residents of many communities tried to provide the "embellishments of civilization" for themselves and their neighbors, the results seemed crude. Perhaps the best case was Milledgeville, where politicians and their wives strived mightily to create a social and intellectual climate worthy of the capital. In the end, however, even the lavish-spending Cobbs (Howell Cobb was governor from 1851-1853) were unable to set a standard of entertaining for the community. Though the "Governor's levee," which heralded the Christmas season, survived as the main social event of the year, it lost much of its festive air when the frugal, teetotaling Baptist Joseph Brown became chief executive in 1857.

Not surprisingly, the social pleasures enjoyed by most Georgians were the less formal, less class-oriented assemblies usually associated with churches, political meetings, or simple, spontaneous gatherings at an inn, tavern, or neighbor's home. In a society where the "common man" prevailed, entertainment which set people apart from each other was often frowned upon, especially by those holding office or seeking it. As a result, the Governor's levee included not only the cream of Georgia society, but, as one who wished a more exclusive company of associates complained, "a great many factory people" and a number of ladies whose gowns "once had colors but which had yielded to the touch of time and water."

Georgia's lack of a "cultured class" largely may have stemmed from limited education. After the Revolutionary War the legislature made a great deal of noise about the need for state-supported schools, but little was done and the task fell to the counties. Most of these did little. Schooling typically lasted but a few years—or in some cases, months—and consisted of the most elementary training. Those who possessed enough money and time could obtain a sound education by attending "academies."

Many of these academies called themselves col-

Left: *In 1838 Presbyterians founded Oglethorpe College near Milledgeville. It failed shortly after the Civil War, in spite of being relocated to the more urban setting of Atlanta. In 1912 Oglethorpe was resurrected as a coeducational institution. Dr. Thornwell Jacobs, its first twentieth-century president, conceived the idea of Oglethorpe's Crypt of Civilization—a time capsule sealed in 1940, to be opened in 8133 A.D.* Courtesy, University of Georgia Libraries Special Collections

Below, left: *Joseph H. Lumpkin founded the University of Georgia Law School and was also the first chief justice of the Georgia Supreme Court. From White,* Historical Collections of Georgia, *1854.* Courtesy, University of Georgia Libraries Special Collections

leges, which occasionally has caused observers to overestimate the state's commitment to higher education. However, some legitimate colleges deserved due attention. At the top of this list was the University of Georgia, endowed by the legislature in 1785 and operating since 1801. Other colleges, most associated with religious denominations, came into being during the 1830s when the Methodists founded Emory, the Baptists founded Mercer, and the Presbyterians founded Oglethorpe. The Methodists also took over Georgia Female College in Macon and renamed it Wesleyan. Augusta boasted a medical college (1828), and Athens, a law school (1859). Thus, many Georgians obtained some education beyond the secondary level.

Despite a dependency on agriculture in general and on cotton in particular, manufacturing interests grew. The War of 1812 demonstrated to Georgians the weakness of their manufacturing base and transportation system. Farmers also needed a reliable means of getting their produce to market, so most of the postwar roads, canals, and railways took agricultural commerce into account. In addition, new routes made economic diversity possible, and though Georgian efforts pale when compared to those of northern states, changing attitudes toward manufacturing occurred.

Westward-moving settlers also began to demand a better means of transport. Turnpike and canal construction dominated the thinking of state leaders dur-

ing the 1820s, but questions of location, maintenance, and funding often delayed or doomed the projects. In the end a combination of private, federal, and state monies underwrote the turnpikes, with private sources carrying most of the burden. Maintenance largely was left to the local populations.

A South Carolina project first introduced Georgians to the new trains. In 1833 a line was built between Charleston and a point just across the Savannah River from Augusta, threatening to deflect the cotton belt's wealth to the Carolina port. That same year the Georgia Railroad, connecting Athens and Augusta, was chartered, and the Central of Georgia (Macon to Savannah) was begun. Though not completed until the 1840s, these lines linked the cotton belt to the coast and gave Georgia's agriculture a number of market advantages. Railroads proved so popular that in 1839 legislators recommended that state funds be used to lay track from the Chattahoochee River in piedmont Georgia to the Tennessee River near Chattanooga. Entirely operated by the state, the Western and Atlantic line was started in 1841 and completed 10 years later. As planned, its southern terminus attracted linkages. In 1845 the Georgia Railroad joined it, and the Atlanta and West Point Railroad began building outward to Alabama. The next year the Central of Georgia arrived, forming the transportation network that was to make Atlanta the hub of a developing region. Other short lines followed, and by 1860 Georgia boasted over 1,200 miles of track.

Like other southern states, Georgia possessed both critics of industry and misguided romantics who believed that the plantation system had created the best of all possible worlds. By mid-century, however, her citizens were also laying the foundation for the industrialism which would usher in the "New South." In the 1850s the state boasted some 40 cotton mills, making her one of the region's leading textile manufacturers. Various factories yielded shoes, iron products, building materials, and other goods. By the eve of the Civil War almost 1,900 industrial establishments employed some 11,500 workers and produced goods worth nearly $17 million. When compared to the value of Georgia's agriculture, that figure seemed small, but growth patterns nevertheless suggested that Georgians were not entirely opposed to industry. Though the classic "southern way of life" rested on the plantation, many Georgians believed there was a place for the factory as well.

# 5

# CIVIL WAR AND

# RECONSTRUCTION

*This unfinished painting by Georgia historian-artist, Wilbur Kurtz, depicts Confederate President Jefferson Davis meeting with his cabinet. Courtesy, Atlanta Historical Society*

Howell Cobb struggled to preserve the Union until Lincoln's election to the presidency. He then became a leader in the secessionist movement in Georgia. Cobb served as president of the provisional Confederate Congress and fought in the Peninsular campaigns. Courtesy, University of Georgia Libraries Special Collections

Robert Toombs, nicknamed the "Unreconstructed Rebel," refused to sign an oath of allegiance after the war, which prevented him from holding elective office. He did, however, remain influential in Georgia politics. Courtesy, University of Georgia Libraries Special Collections

Politics in antebellum Georgia focused mainly on local issues and personalities, although a number of Georgia's leaders, men like Howell Cobb and Alexander H. Stephens, moved into the broader political arena. Less extreme and inflammatory in word and deed than their colleagues from other states, they maintained a moderate position on the issues which threatened to divide the nation. Georgia undeservingly became associated with this rational political approach. As the question of the expansion of slavery came to the forefront, white Georgians doggedly protected their peculiar institution; and they used states' rights as their principal weapon against a growing Northern majority. Georgia citizens thus became increasingly regional in outlook and defensive in posture.

To say that slavery was the only issue with which Georgians were concerned, however, would grossly oversimplify a tremendously complex situation. States' rights remained a political principle as old as the nation, and it claimed both northern and southern advocates. White southerners also raised political and philosophical questions about the aggressively capitalistic way of life they perceived to be developing in the north. They argued that an agricul-

tural society offered man far more benefits than one based on manufacturing. Yet, when southerners used states' rights to defend slavery and their way of life, human bondage became the central issue.

For a time, however, citizens seemed willing to meet their northern counterparts half way. When debates over the admission of California, slave trade in the District of Columbia, and the fugitive slave law threatened to divide the nation, Georgians Cobb, Stephens, and Robert Toombs worked for a congressional compromise; they also called on delegates attending a state convention to help resolve these problematic issues. The resulting "Georgia Platform" cooled the national crisis. Yet, Georgia leaders asserted that they had gone as far as they were willing to go in accommodating northern antislavery attitudes.

The rise of the Republican party, which opposed the expansion of slavery and threatened the South with permanent minority status, heightened regional fears and contributed to a realignment on the local political scene. In Georgia this led to the unexpected election of Joseph E. Brown as governor in 1857. A north Georgia judge with yeoman farmer roots, Brown parlayed a strong states' rights stance and a

common man image into a winning combination. Though not yet a committed secessionist, the new governor believed that such a course of action was legal, and he considered it a viable option if all else failed.

Meanwhile, Republican strength was growing in the North and, at much the same time, southerners found the northern wing of the Democratic party less willing to listen to their regional concerns. All this came to a head in 1860, when the Democrats met in Charleston to select their presidential candidate. The convention refused to adopt a platform protecting slavery in the territories, and eight southern states, including most of the Georgia delegation, walked out. In the aftermath two conventions were held. Northern Democrats selected Stephen A. Douglas of Illinois as their presidential candidate and, in an effort to present themselves as a national party, picked Herschel V. Johnson, a Georgia unionist, as his running mate. The southern wing of the party chose John C. Breckinridge of Kentucky and Joseph Lane of Oregon to head their ticket.

November's election revealed Georgia to be a badly divided state. Although Breckinridge received the most votes (51,893), John Bell of Tennessee, standard bearer of the hastily organized but more moderate Constitutional Union party, ran a strong second (42,855). Douglas picked up enough votes to deny Breckinridge a majority, so the decision went to the legislature, which gave the front-runner all of the state's electoral votes. However, it was Abraham Lincoln—the Republican candidate with almost no support in the South—who won the presidency. His election presented Georgia with a dilemma. Some citizens believed the state should secede immediately (as

South Carolina had done on December 20), but others felt that the southern states should act together, and therefore Georgia should wait. To settle the issue the Georgia legislature called for the election of a convention to decide which course to take.

Delegate selection demonstrated regional polarization. Secessionists proved strongest in the cities and the plantation belt, while unionists of varying shades held a majority in the mountains and in the poorer areas populated by yeoman farmers. The secessionists carried the day. Immediate secession candidates received just over 50,000 votes, while their opponents polled some 37,000.

The convention met from the middle to the end of January 1861. Most of the early votes were fairly close, but when the issue of secession finally came to the floor, it passed overwhelmingly. A short time later delegates were chosen to go to Montgomery, Alabama, where representatives from other seceding states would meet to create the Confederacy.

Georgia's leaders had doubted that secession could be accomplished peacefully, for the same legislature that organized the convention also allocated one million dollars for defense and sought to raise 10,000 troops. It was not long before suspicions were realized. On April 12 Confederate batteries opened fire on Fort Sumter in Charleston Harbor, and the Civil War began. Georgia volunteers rushed to the Southern standard; by June some 18,000 recruits entered military service.

Problems between the state and the new nation immediately began to develop, however. Although Georgians were prominent in organizing the Confederate States of America (Howell Cobb served as president of the Montgomery convention; T.R.R. Cobb as principal author of the Confederate constitution; Alexander H. Stephens as the young nation's vice-president; and Robert Toombs as secretary of state) it was not long before leaders opposed the central government's conduct of political affairs. Heading the list of critics was Governor Brown, who viewed Davis' centralized policies as a threat. Brown charted a course that favored Georgia and Georgians, and because of his generally uncooperative attitude toward collective Confederate goals, he often has been cited by those who argue that states' rights gave birth to the Confederacy but also led to the South's defeat. Supported in varying degrees by other state leaders, Brown did what he felt was best for his people, and

they responded by reelecting him throughout the war.

Finding that Georgia possessed more volunteers than arms, Governor Brown forbade his troops from carrying weapons out of the state. Later in the conflict he refused to allow soldiers from other states to use Georgia munitions when serving there. As the war dragged on, Brown also opposed conscription and exempted state civil and military officials—known as "Joe Brown's pets"—from Confederate service. Finally, he refused to enforce laws on impressment and certain in-kind taxes.

Governor Brown's primary concern was the defense of the Georgia coast. Federal forces occupied Tybee Island at the mouth of the Savannah River in November 1861, and other sea islands came under enemy control during the following months. Attempting to keep the port of Savannah open, the Confederate government sent Robert E. Lee to oversee coastal defenses. Lee's efforts proved fruitless. In the spring of 1862 the Union made its move against Fort Pulaski, which guarded the channel leading to Savannah. After bypassing the garrison and cutting it off from support, federal forces opened fire from Tybee Island with new rifled artillery. The bombardment lasted only one day. Pulaski's massive masonry walls crumbled, and on April 11 the garrison surrendered.

The attack on Savannah—expected after Pulaski's fall—never came. Perhaps it would have been overkill. The surrender already had closed the river, and with it, Georgia's principal port. Federal forces instead chose to raid along the coast while Georgians responded by trying to block the rivers which might be used as avenues of invasion. Meanwhile, Union troops occupying the sea islands organized slaves from abandoned plantations into colonies, and an early phase of the Reconstruction was set in motion. The summer of 1863 saw increased federal activity, with attacks launched against Darien at the mouth of the Altamaha, and Fort McAllister at the Ogeechee. McAllister withstood repeated assaults, but Darien was taken and burned, an act which Georgians viewed as a warning of what could be expected from the enemy.

Citizens residing inland had little direct contact with the fighting until mid-1864. In 1863, the Western and Atlantic Railroad became the target of a Union operation in which some 1,600 mounted troops under Colonel Abel D. Streight rode into north Georgia. They were met by Confederate General Nathan B. Forrest's hastily organized, poorly armed, and generally inexperienced force. With less than half the number of Union troops, the southerners managed to push the enemy back into Alabama where they surrendered. It was one of the few bright spots in what was becoming an increasingly bleak situation.

Like the Confederacy itself, Georgia perpetually faced the problem of financing the war. The state first sold bonds, then raised taxes, and finally imposed new ones, including levies on profit and income. Most of the money raised went directly into the war effort and toward assisting the wounded and their families, the widows, and the orphans.

In some ways, the war stimulated the economy. Industry and manufacturing grew, spurred by the army's needs and state appropriations designed to promote and encourage military-related activity. Atlanta became the supply center for Confederate troops in the east, as well as a major producer of rails and armor plate; Columbus manufactured gunboats and engines; Augusta's powder works were said to be the largest in the world; Macon boasted the Schofield Ironworks; and fall-line towns continued as textile and clothing centers. But even with Governor Brown's exemption of skilled workers from military service, trained labor remained a critical concern, as was the shortage of capital needed to build new factories or expand old ones.

Georgia's railroads faced increased demands on their limited resources. The network of lines serving her so well before the conflict made Georgia a pivotal state in supplying Virginia, Tennessee, and western troops. Georgia also became a critical link in the Confederacy's communication scheme.

Eventually repairs and replacement became a major concern, and the state's factories simply could not meet the demand for rails and other materials. Compounding the problem was a lack of skilled workers; whereas textiles and other light industries could use women and children to take up slack, the railroads could not. As a result Georgia turned to the labor supply that had been the backbone of her prewar economy, and soon black crews and section hands worked the lines. Their employment on the railroads and in other critical wartime industries clearly showed that it was slavery that retarded black progress, not lack of skill as some whites argued when defending the plantation system.

Most black Georgians stayed on farms, however, for despite industrial needs, agriculture remained the mainstay of the state's economy. But the war greatly taxed the cotton empire. Land and labor were being channeled into food production for soldiers at the front and civilians at home. With Governor Brown urging a cutback in cotton planting and with a legislative act restricting cultivation to no more than three acres for every farm laborer (which did not go as far as the governor wanted), production fell from 700,000 bales in 1860 to 60,000 bales two years later. This downward trend continued for the rest of the conflict. Georgia farmers diversified and subsequently became one of the South's principal suppliers of foodstuffs and a major source for the Virginia armies until the Union invasion of 1864.

With the continued struggle, many black Georgians experienced a measure of freedom previously unknown. Slaves often found themselves with less supervision—and therefore more control over their own lives—when their masters left for the front. Some blacks continued to serve much as they had before, but others adopted a policy of passive resistance to their tasks. Still others flatly refused work assignments, and when the Union invasion came in 1864, hundreds left their homes to follow the victors to freedom. Responses varied as widely as the people and the living conditions, yet increased resistance showed that the South's peculiar institution was changing.

Although the casual observer might have noted few differences in Georgians' day-to-day existence, the conflict slowly but surely took its toll from 1861 onward. Primary and secondary schools continued much as before, but only Mercer among men's colleges was able to keep its doors open. Conversely, Wesleyan actually increased its enrollment as southern women sought to train themselves to cope with whatever came from the war. Despite the need for physicians, the medical college in Augusta was converted into a hospital to care for the wounded. Social life also quickly focused on activities related to the war effort. Churches raised supplies, sent religious tracts and Bibles to the armies, recruited chaplains, and did what they could to provide soldiers with the homey touches so necessary for morale. Aid to the returning wounded and their families, war widows, and orphans further consumed the energies of those who staffed the home front.

In anticipation of an attack, Confederate fortifications ringed the city of Atlanta in 1864. These cannons were intended to defend the southwest portion of the city. Courtesy, Atlanta Historical Society

Then, early in 1864, Georgians began to learn about the war firsthand. Chattanooga had surrendered to a Union army during the previous autumn, and the enemy moved into the northwest corner of the state. Confederate forces briefly checked this advance with a victory at Chickamauga, but in November the South suffered a crushing defeat at Missionary Ridge outside Chattanooga. The road to Georgia subsequently seemed open and inviting.

The man chosen to lead the invasion of Georgia was General William T. Sherman, and in May 1864 his army of nearly 100,000 stood ready. Confederate General Joseph E. Johnston led the opposing forces—fewer than 45,000 men. The Union objective was clear: capture Atlanta. At the hub of Georgia's railroad lines, Atlanta served as the supply depot for what remained of the Confederate war effort in the east. Equally important, the city was situated deep in the heart of Dixie, and her fall would render a significant psychological setback for southern civilian and military morale. Atlanta also would give the Union army a base from which to conduct operations in Georgia, South Carolina, and Alabama. Union strategists knew what hung in the balance, and so did the Confederates.

In May 1864 Sherman moved south. Johnston took up a strong position at Dalton, but the Confederates were outflanked, and then were attacked at Resaca, where they sustained heavy losses. Retreating down the Western and Atlantic Railroad (their principal supply route), Johnston tried to avoid any battle where the Union forces could take advantage of their superior numbers. The result was a series of flanking movements which kept the armies close to each other but prevented a major engagement.

Finally, the Union commander decided the time had come to throw this strength against Johnston. On June 27 he directed a frontal assault at the well-entrenched Confederates at Kennesaw Mountain, about 20 miles northwest of Atlanta. It proved to be a costly decision, for when the battle ended, Sherman had little to show for the 3,000 casualties suffered by his forces. Unwilling to renew the attack, the Union general flanked Johnston's army again and the Confederate troops withdrew to below the Chattahoochee. Sherman had moved his army some 100 miles in 74 days, and in the process had suffered 25,000 casualties. Johnston's losses were considerably less, but his troops remained more difficult to replace. By July 9, 1864, the two armies confronted

*Shelling destroyed the Ponder house on the northwest line of fortifications which circled Atlanta. This picture is dated 1864. Courtesy, Atlanta Historical Society*

each other across the Chattahoochee River and the Battles for Atlanta were about to begin.

Confederate morale remained high despite all the retreating. Atlanta was well defended and everyone assumed that a long siege would be difficult to sustain. But President Jefferson Davis, impatient with Johnston's failure to take the offensive, replaced him with General John B. Hood. With Davis' mandate to fight, Hood took charge of the army on July 17 and three days later ordered his troops to attack the federal force as they crossed Peachtree Creek. The assault failed, and when the day ended the Confederates had sustained nearly 1,000 more casualties than the Union troops. Peachtree Creek was followed, two days later, by fighting east of the city. This is the actual Battle of Atlanta depicted in the painting at the Grant Park cyclorama in Atlanta. Like the fighting that preceded it, the battle went badly for the South. A third clash near Ezra Church, west of the city, took place less than a week later. It represented yet another defeat for the Confederacy. In the short time he had been in command, General John B. Hood counted almost 15,000 casualties. Aware that his army could not continue to sustain such losses, he withdrew into Atlanta's defenses, and the siege began.

During the following weeks, Union forces took up positions around much of Atlanta, and their batteries pounded military and civilian targets alike. The beseiged citizens adopted what one observer called "a very ingenious mode of protecting themselves by digging deep holes like cisterns and covering them over sufficiently thick to ensure safety"—in one part of town "every yard . . . had one large enough to contain the entire family." On the line of battle the two sides were often within shouting distance of each other and during a rare ceasefire, they left their trenches to talk and exchange articles. "It is strange," a Union officer wrote, "that men who meet in deadly strife today should tomorrow meet and extend the right hand of fellowship to one another but nevertheless it is so."

The shelling and encirclement continued until August 26, when the Union army turned south to cut the railroad running to Macon—Atlanta's last supply line. Left with little choice, Hood evacuated the city on September 1, 1864. Since taking command General Hood had lost over 27,000 men and the city of Atlanta. Meanwhile, Sherman ordered the approximately 1,600 remaining Atlantans to leave; then he resupplied, rested his army, and prepared for the next phase.

In November Sherman was ready. He ordered all of the city's primary buildings—factories, warehouses, railroad facilities, and others—burned to the ground. When his army marched out, only some 400 dwellings stood. Then with 5,000 cavalry and 57,000 infantrymen, Sherman began the "march through Georgia." There was little to oppose him. On November 22 the state capital was taken, and a mock legislature repealed the act of secession. Two days later the army left after burning a number of war-related facilities (the Capitol, the executive mansion, and the town were untouched, however). Then Sherman's army regrouped near Sandersville and proceeded to cut a path through the center of Georgia. Farms and plantations were burned—despite specific orders forbidding attacks on personal property. Perhaps the greatest impact on the civilian population came from the fact that the invading army—as well as southern soldiers—had to live off the land, which had a disheartening effect on the morale of its people.

By early December Sherman was rapidly approaching Savannah, and on December 21 Union

A ring of fortifications defended Atlanta against the Yankee invaders. From this position, near the present site of Georgia Tech, two other fortified points could be seen along the horizon. Courtesy, Atlanta Historical Society

troops actually entered the city. "I beg to present you as a Christmas present," Sherman wired to Lincoln, "the City of Savannah." In its march through Georgia the Union Army presided over the destruction of more than $100 million worth of property, encompassing some 40 central Georgia counties. Everyone could see the end in sight. Meanwhile, Sherman's army rested in Savannah until February 1, 1865, and then headed into South Carolina.

A short time later a Union force of about 13,000 cavalrymen under General James H. Wilson invaded Georgia from Alabama, and on April 16—a week after Lee delivered his army to Grant at Appomattox—Columbus fell. Following the destruction of local industries, Union troops moved on to Macon, where General Howell Cobb and some 3,000 militia surrendered on April 20. A few weeks later Governor Brown yielded the state's remaining forces, mostly old men and boys, and federal military authorities took charge. For Georgia, Reconstruction had begun.

It is impossible to briefly summarize what war and defeat generally meant to white Georgian supporters of the Confederacy, but the picture becomes clearer perhaps when one examines more personal cases. In April 1861, for example, the Baldwin Blues,

a 71-man company from Milledgeville, left the capital on an early morning train. Despite the hour a "thousand citizens" turned out, speeches were made, flowers strewn, and tears shed. The Blues joined Lee's army in Virginia and subsequently fought in all the major battles there. Casualties were high from the beginning, but until 1863 replacements were quickly found. After that a $50 bounty had to be offered; even then recruits came slowly, as the war took a fearful toll. Only seven of the original company were left to surrender at Appomattox, and just two of the ten commanding officers escaped injury, capture, or death. One hundred fifty-two men served in the Baldwin Blues. Ultimately, 35 remained on the muster roll: 14 as prisoners, 11 on leave or sick, and two listed as absent. All the rest had either died, been wounded, been captured, or deserted. Similar accounts could be given for other units from other Georgia towns.

Not all Georgians mourned the fall of the Confederacy, though. Black Georgians welcomed the conquering Union army, and many left their homes to join it on its march to the sea. Their response to freedom was as varied as the circumstances under which they lived: thousands deserted the plantations for towns and cities; many stayed on to work as hired hands; some were unable to leave or had no idea of where to go; and others squatted on abandoned land in hopes that emancipation would bring property and true independence. Common to all, however, were the convictions that freedom was better than slavery and that a new and better day was dawning.

Many white Georgians accepted the defeat of the South with an attitude quite different from the defiant "fergit hell!" so often associated with the unreconstructed rebel. From the start of the war, some had felt that secession was a mistake at best. As a result they were less than enthusiastic in their support of the Confederacy. Now these men, who would be called "scalawags" by the diehards, proved ready to help restore federal authority so that they could get back to business. Furthermore, the war's suffering and privation had drained many Confederate supporters; by 1865 they were willing to surrender. Though the latter attitude surfaced in most quarters, it appeared perhaps most pronounced among the troops themselves. With defeat staring them in the face and news from their families increasingly bleak, vast numbers of soldiers voted with their feet. It is estimated that in 1865 nearly half of the Georgians subject to military duty were absent from the army. For these men and their loved ones the end could not come soon enough.

Thus, most Georgians accepted defeat and willingly rejoined the Union. In October 1865 a constitutional convention—generally employing prewar voter qualifications, but excluding Confederate civil and military officials—was chosen by the electorate. With conservative unionists dominant, the assembly abolished slavery, repudiated secession, and dissolved the war debt. The next month Georgians elected unionist Charles J. Jenkins as their governor, along with a legislature which quickly ratified the Thirteenth Amendment, freeing slaves. United States representatives and senators also were chosen, and Georgia appeared to be reconstructed—at least to Georgians.

Serious problems remained, however. Freed blacks had not been granted full civil rights. For example, they could not testify against whites, nor could they vote. Other relics of the defeated system also remained in place. In Georgia and other southern states, the Democratic party seemed ready to rise to its prewar power, a potentially significant setback for Republicans on the national level. Fearing a Democratic resurgency and arguing that President Andrew Johnson's interpretation of Reconstruction bolstered the South at the expense of the newly acquired rights of freemen, radical Republicans moved to seize control. Their sincerity on both of the above counts is still debated today, but they nevertheless sealed their victory in 1867 by passing the Military Reconstruction Acts.

The next few years proved to be trying times for Georgia and the nation, leaving a bitter legacy which shaped the future of both races. The state's refusal to ratify the Fourteenth Amendment was cited as proof that she was not reconstructed; therefore, Georgia became part of the Third Military District headed by General John Pope. Under his administration and that of his successor, General George G. Meade, a new constitution was written and the Fourteenth Amendment ratified. Conflicts ensued, however, resulting in the removal of the governor and a number of state officials, all of whom were replaced briefly by military officers. Still, voices of moderation—sometimes heard and heeded—spared Georgia much of the dislocation and dissension felt in her sister states.

Georgia effectively went through three reconstructions (one presidential and two congressional) before finally returning to the Union with full privileges. This process left behind it deep racial divisions, as blacks were often blamed for whites' suffering. In addition, a distrust of the federal government in general (and of Republicans in particular) would last for over a century. Reconstruction politics yielded fraud, intimidation, and violence on both sides, and the Ku Klux Klan first appeared during this era. With the election of a Democratic legislature in 1870, Georgia "redeemed" itself in the eyes of native whites, but the short-lived political participation of black Georgians came to an end. Thirty-two blacks had been voted into the 1868 legislature, only to be expelled by the white majority. Nearly a year and a half passed before they regained their seats. Although blacks played little real part in government during Reconstruction, the experience temporarily gave them hopes for the future. Yet, the election of 1870 demonstrated that Reconstruction and its promises of participation indeed had ended. For the state's black citizens the new day they thought was dawning still appeared a long way off.

# 6

# FARMS, FACTORIES,

# AND FACTIONS

# IN THE NEW SOUTH

*Scenes like this one in 1913 Carroll County explain what is meant by the term, someone is "in tall cotton." Courtesy, Georgia Department of Archives and History*

Above: *This cotton press squeezes loose cotton into tightly packed bales of about 500 pounds for more efficient handling during shipment. From King, The Great South, 1875, courtesy, Atlanta Historical Society*

Left: *The origin of the term "cracker," which characterizes poor rural whites, is unknown, although it appears very early in Georgia history. From King, The Great South, 1875, courtesy, Atlanta Historical Society*

The devastation and disruption of the Civil War tore apart the economic pillars of Georgia and those of her fellow Confederate states. Besides totally changing the nature of the region's labor system, the termination of slavery instantly wiped out millions of dollars in assets. Limited as it had been, the South's industrial base also struggled to convert from military to civilian needs. A new political order, dominated by the business-minded Bourbons of the planter-merchant class, further arose as the state underwent difficult economic changes.

The most immediate postwar transformation facing Georgia proved to be the restructuring of the labor system. Some effort was made to restore a semblance of the plantation system by paying wages to the former slaves. Yet, the severe lack of capital and black resistance to such direct control made it difficult for many large landowners to maintain a sufficient labor force.

By the end of the 1860s, a system of tenancy—especially crop tenancy—had begun to dominate the southern agricultural landscape. The overwhelming majority of both the white and black populations consisted of uneducated farm laborers, and though some owned land, the majority were propertyless. The 1900 census counted almost half of Georgia's population as black, but these citizens claimed under five percent of farm acreage. The great plantation families had lost some of their land to banks and other investors, but little fell to the ownership of poor dirt farmers. In the mountain and upper piedmont areas of north Georgia, farm ownership was more widespread than in the plantation regions. Largely self-sufficient, these mountain yeomen usually raised very few cash crops on their small valley plots.

The tenancy system had numerous variations. Some farmers, mainly whites, possessed the agricultural skill and money-management experience necessary to become cash tenants, i.e. those who simply paid rent for their land and otherwise controlled their own affairs. This approach proved impractical for most farming Georgians; sharecropping, therefore, emerged as an alternative.

At one time the theory of sharecropping was based on dividing the produce, mostly cotton, into thirds: a third for the land which, usually included a house; a third for the capital investment in mules, implements, seed, and fertilizer; and a third for the labor of the tenant. By the mid- to late-1870s, however, the typical Georgia tenant was supplying only

Above: *Cotton was shipped from Savannah to mills in the northeast. From King,* The Great South, *1875, courtesy, Atlanta Historical Society*

Below: *Savannah has been Georgia's most important port since its founding. Georgia cotton, pressed into bales, passed through Savannah on the way to the cloth mills of the world. From King,* The Great South, *1875, courtesy, Atlanta Historical Society*

the labor of his family and was dividing the crop half-and-half with his landlord. With a myriad minor modifications, this fifty-fifty division survived as the dominant arrangement well into the twentieth century. Legally, the sharecropper was not an independent farmer at all; he remained a simple laborer who happened to be paid with cotton rather than currency.

Sharecropping, nevertheless, provided a feeling of self-sufficiency for the farmer, an aspect of the system especially relished by the freedmen. As slaves, the blacks had usually lived under tight supervision in cabins close to the main house; even though sharecropping largely confined them to primitive, one-room shacks, the ability to spread out across the old plantation proved a welcome change.

Cotton growing was highly labor-intensive, involving long hours for the tenant and his wife and children, but the work only took six to eight months, which allowed for visiting and other activities. Fishing and hunting became popular sports since they provided both recreation and food for the table. Still, the appearance of independence was largely illusory; the tenants remained trapped in a limited economic order, with little hope of bettering themselves and their families.

Above: *Richard Peters, railroad pioneer, changed his city's name from Marthasville to Atlanta. He kept a model farm on the outskirts of the city. From Reed, Reed's History of Atlanta, 1889, courtesy, Atlanta Historical Society*

Above: *At the turn of the century, cotton bales often covered the Savannah wharf, which served the Central Railroad and the Ocean Steamship Line. Courtesy, Georgia Department of Archives and History*

Below: *Cotton came to market at Carrollton, Georgia, in mule-drawn wagons. Notice the Confederate monument in this 1919 view of the town square. Courtesy, Georgia Department of Archives and History*

Above: *During Reconstruction, illiterate ex-slaves were often exploited by cynical politicians of both political parties. From King,* The Great South, *1875, courtesy, Atlanta Historical Society*

Landlords and creditors insisted that the cash crop consume virtually every acre, leaving practically no space for gardening or stock maintenance. Editors and experts often advocated agricultural diversification, and people such as Richard Peters, an Atlanta real estate promoter and north Georgia farmer, made great strides in developing a wide range of crops and livestock. Still, these pioneers were bucking the trend. Most farmers managed to grow some corn for food and feed, but in the last two decades of the nineteenth century, over 40 percent of Georgia's cultivated acreage was devoted to cotton—an even higher percentage than before the war.

Both tenants and landlords conformed to the crop lien system directly associated with sharecropping. The local merchant advanced credit to the landowner for seed, fertilizer, and implements, while the tenant obtained assistance in the purchase of corn meal, yard goods, household items, and the like. Often the tenant received his supplies or cash advances directly from the landlord rather than from the country store. This makeshift system remained the only source of credit available to most Georgians; as late as 1894 three-fourths of the counties in the state had no incorporated banks at all.

To secure loans, the merchant obtained liens on the anticipated yield. He was paid when the crops were sold. If prices tumbled or production proved less than expected, the merchant might get all of the output, plus an additional lien against the coming year. Agricultural prices steadily declined from the mid-1870s into the 1890s, and many Georgians found themselves in an endless circle of debt. The tenant felt even greater pressure when the merchant, cotton gin owner, and landlord were one and the same, which was a fairly frequent occurrence.

Agricultural historian Gilbert Fite used census records to fashion a description of the typical circa-1880 central Georgia sharecropper. He and his family cultivated approximately 13-40 acres. Cotton grew on half or more of the improved land, and the balance usually held corn. A bale of cotton weighed about 500 pounds. With production averaging about one-third bale per acre and with cotton selling for nine cents per pound in the 1880s, each acre yielded just over $13. Thus, a small Georgia sharecropper tending 20 acres could expect to gross about $260, half of which he owed to the landlord. In addition to the cotton, many farmers owned a few hogs,

maybe a cow or two, and some chickens.

The cycle of dependency was aggravated by the fact that in order to purchase their inventories, merchants and planters themselves owed much to bankers and wholesalers. Many southern lenders in turn were obligated to northern financial institutions. Therefore, the crop lien system entrapped

whites and blacks alike.

Many Georgians believed that the Empire state could only break out of its economic doldrums by increasing industrialization. John F. Hanson trumpeted such New South ideology in his *Macon Telegraph*, as did Patrick Walsh in the *Augusta Chronicle*; yet, no one proved a more eloquent or effective spokesman for this viewpoint than Henry W. Grady, the youthful and vigorous editor of the *Atlanta Constitution*. During his short life Henry Grady served as the principal propagandist for the so-called "New South," a term he supposedly coined in an 1874 *Atlanta Daily Herald* editorial and popularized in a famous speech to the New England Society 12 years later. "As long as we manufacture nothing," Grady once wrote, "and rely on the shops and mills and factories of other sections for everything we use, our section must remain dependent and poor." The invitation to northern capital did not include a welcome for northern mores, for Grady and other New South spokesmen had no intention of threatening Georgia's racial caste system.

The most significant efforts to boost the state's industries were three world's fair-type regional exhibitions staged in Atlanta. The first, the International

Above: *As a transportation center, Atlanta linked Georgia to the rest of the nation. From Clarke,* Illustrated History of Atlanta, *1881, courtesy, Atlanta Historical Society*

Facing page, top: *In the fall of 1887, shortly after this picture was made, President Grover Cleveland addressed this Atlanta crowd from the Markham House Hotel. The curved roof of the railroad terminal is visible in the foreground. Courtesy, Atlanta Historical Society*

Facing page, bottom: *Henry Grady, editor of the Atlanta Consti-tution, popularized the idea of a "New South," where commerce and industry would replace plantation agriculture as the centerpiece of the southern economy. Courtesy, Atlanta Historical Society*

Cotton Exposition of 1881, featured over a thousand displays from dozens of states and seven foreign na-tions. Six years later the smaller Piedmont Exposition drew a visit from President Grover Cleveland. Esti-mated attendance was 200,000.

The greatest of Atlanta's three extravaganzas proved to be the Cotton States and International Ex-position of 1895, which drew 800,000 visitors in three months. Held on the same site as the 1887 fair, this event was much expanded, with attractions such as Buffalo Bill's Wild West Show and John Philip Sousa's band. Visitors again included President Cleve-land. Exposition organizers provided a special Negro building, which highlighted black contributions to the southern economy, and Booker T. Washington's speech at the fair helped make him the most noted black leader of the day. In the early 1950s, Atlanta's official historian Franklin M. Garrett observed, "The . . . Exposition . . . gave Atlanta more of a boost than any single event, before or since."

As the names of the two major fairs indicate, cot-ton continued to be king, and its mills dominated Georgia manufacturing. Still, most of Georgia's raw cotton was shipped to textile manufacturers outside the state, although by 1900 the state claimed 111 cot-

ton mills. When the Georgia School of Technology—later Georgia Tech—opened its doors in Atlanta in 1888, the state's commitment to industrial growth truly became evident.

Still, even the boldest efforts did not lead to the anticipated industrial transformation. To be sure, there was impressive recovery from the destruction of the war, but by the end of the century Georgia's tiny portion of the national manufacturing output did not yet quite match 1860 levels. The manufac-turing, mining, and mechanical sectors of the econ-omy employed less than 10 percent of the popula-tion, and almost all industries concentrated on processing Georgia's main raw materials: food, cot-ton, and trees.

The main manufacturing cities continued to be the fall line trio of Augusta, Macon, and Columbus, but many cotton mills were actually located in rural settings. Whether city- or country-based, the mills spawned company-owned villages. There, most of the workers and their families lived in small, frame dwellings often called "shotgun houses" because they were only about as wide as the pattern made by buck-shot. The so-called "lint heads" who toiled in the mills sometimes clocked 70 hours a week; often

Left: *Street railways made the expansion of Atlanta suburbs possible. This horse-drawn trolley moves onto a bridge over Clear Creek. The route of this streetcar line is now Ponce de Leon Avenue; Penn Avenue occupies the location of the creek. The bridge in this image is dated to 1874. Courtesy, Atlanta Historical Society*

Facing page: *When the Kimball House opened in 1870, the Constitution found its yellow and brown exterior "handsome and ornamental" and its accommodations "luxurious, splendid, palatial." Other amenities included separate steam-powered elevators for passengers and baggage. The hotel cost more than $600,000 to build and furnish. From Clarke,* Illustrated History of Atlanta, *1881, courtesy, Atlanta Historical Society*

shopped at overpriced company stores; and occasionally worshiped in company-built churches. Women and children—some in their preteen years—made up a majority of the textile labor force in the 1890s. Southern wages were as much as 40 percent lower than those in the North. These low labor costs attracted northern investment, especially in the late 1890s.

To transport southern cotton, lumber, and other products, and to import finished goods from the north, Georgia considerably expanded her prewar railroad network of nearly 1,500 miles. Atlanta's rise to urban predominance was due largely to its key role in the state and regional train system. Immediately after Southern surrender, Georgia railroads stood in financial and physical shambles, but by 1890 total mileage exceeded 4,500.

The depression of the 1890s curtailed railroad expansion; several railroad corporations collapsed. Great new combinations, such as the Southern Railway Company organized by J.P. Morgan and other northern financiers, arose out of the turmoil. Columbus native Samuel Spencer became the firm's first president. Its main regional rivals were the Atlantic Coast Line, the Louisville & Nashville, and the Seaboard Air Line. Improved transportation boosted economic development all over the state.

Because the Republicans had dominated Congress during the Civil War and Reconstruction, most white Georgians resented them and clung to the Democratic party. Democrats obtained a legislative majority in 1871 and captured the governorship the following year; they never again relinquished control of either. Despite challenges from Populists and occasional dissent within their own ranks, the so-called Bourbon Democrats ruled state politics for generations, maintaining their grip through effective manipulation of seemingly contradictory ideas. They glorified the "Lost Cause," but worked for sectional reconciliation. While preaching white supremacy, they utilized black votes to defeat political rivals. Finally, they sought to industrialize the South without seriously threatening the economically established planter class and county seat elites.

Just before the Democratic legislature convened in November 1871, Republican Governor Rufus B. Bullock resigned and fled the state to avoid impeachment over alleged railroad mismanagement and other corruption. Depite his New York origins and Republican affiliation, Bullock was not really a carpet-

bagger. He had moved to Augusta in 1857 to work for an express company and served the Confederacy as a lieutenant colonel in the quartermaster corps. After the war Bullock turned to banking and railroad investments, entering politics as a means of improving the state's ability to attract northern capital.

Meanwhile, Bullock's close associate, hotel builder and railroad magnate Hannibal I. Kimball, also left the state on account of railroad scandals. Since Kimball's involvement with Georgia and the South did not begin until after the war, he sometimes was tagged as a "carpetbagger." Yet, the transportation mogul was welcomed by Atlanta businessmen as long as he steered clear of politics. In fact, the availability of Kimball's Opera House as a temporary capitol building proved to be a key factor in the successful effort by Atlanta's boosters and Republican reconstruction officials to transfer the seat of government from Milledgeville in 1867.

Indeed, Atlanta and the state would soon welcome back both Kimball and Bullock. Bullock was acquitted of the charges against him, and Kimball was never even indicted. The former governor went on to serve his city as president of the Atlanta Cotton Factory Company, the Commercial Club, and the chamber of commerce. Following business reverses, Bullock returned to New York in the 1890s, where he died.

Similarly, Kimball chaired the International Cotton Exposition of 1881, rebuilt his Kimball House Hotel in 1885 after fire destroyed the 1870 original, and invested widely in real estate. Henry Grady once declared that the magnate could talk "more enterprise in a minute than most any other Georgian can talk in a whole day."

With Reconstruction effectively over, the most resistant Democrats, led by Robert Toombs, set out to remove the last vestiges of Republican rule by rewriting the state constitution in 1877. Blessed with a knack for making money and cursed with an addiction to alcohol, Toombs had been a state legislator, congressman, and United States senator before the war. He served the Confederacy as secretary of state and then as a brigadier general before angrily resigning and becoming a colonel in the Georgia State Guards. Along with fellow Georgians Alexander H. Stephens and Joseph E. Brown, Toombs was a strong critic of Jefferson Davis.

After Southern surrender, this Georgian leader

proved in a December 1877 referendum, reflected agriculturalist suspicion of state government and was a blow to the more industrially oriented Bourbons. Its provisions prevented the General Assembly from appropriating money or providing tax breaks for economic development; furthermore, the new constitution laid the groundwork for subsequent railroad regulation. Although a public school system had been authorized in 1868, Toombs' document limited allocations to elementary education only.

Unable to work their will on the new constitution, the Bourbons nevertheless dominated the major state offices through the triumvirate of Confederate generals John B. Gordon and Alfred H. Colquitt and wartime Governor Joseph E. Brown. Henry Grady was the publicist and strategist for this trio. As governor, Colquitt appointed Brown to the U.S. Senate when Gordon resigned in 1879 to take an arranged railroad job. Upon the death of Senator Benjamin H. Hill four years later, Colquitt went to the Senate. The aging Alexander H. Stephens, vice president of the Confederacy, succeeded Colquitt as governor. The next elected governor, Henry D. McDaniel, was a compromise between the Atlanta and Macon factions. Grady had worked hard to prevent

stoutly refused to seek a presidential pardon, which prevented him from holding public office. Nevertheless, Toombs was the driving force behind the effort to dispose of the 1868 constitution, which he regarded as "the handiwork of Negroes, thieves and Yankees." The resulting document, strongly ap-

the nomination of Augustus O. Bacon, the Macon favorite. In 1886 Grady again thwarted Bacon, this time by engineering the nomination and election of Gordon, whose face bore the politically valuable scar of a Yankee-inflicted wound. General Gordon's candidacy was launched when he accompanied the aged and ailing Jefferson Davis on a Grady-arranged tour that included Atlanta and Savannah. The ascendency of the Atlanta-oriented Bourbon triumvirate was now complete—they held both Senate seats and the governorship.

A significant political challenge to Bourbon rule arose out of the economic distress found in the agricultural sector during the last decade of the century. As early as the 1870s the Grange movement (National Grange of the Patrons of Husbandry) had attracted some Georgia farmers to its program of cooperative marketing and railroad regulation. For various reasons, however, the Grange faded away, and the loosely organized but broader Farmer's Alliance took its place. The more than 100,000 Georgia Alliancemen were becoming explicitly political by 1890.

At first, Georgia Democrats fell all over themselves to appease the Alliance. In 1890 all ten con-

gressmen, both major candidates for governor, and most of the General Assembly professed to support the new movement's demands. Even General John B. Gordon took enough of an Alliance stance to ensure that the legislators would send him to the United States Senate when he left the governorship. The "Farmers' Legislature" of 1891 expanded railroad, bank, and fertilizer regulation and increased public school appropriations. It did not turn out to be the agent of reform that the more extreme Alliancemen wanted, however. Realizing their constraints within the Bourbon-dominated Democratic party, many Georgia Alliance members joined their brothers from other southern and western states in forming the People's party, whose members were generally called Populists.

The leading Georgia Populist and one of the party's most important national spokesmen was Thomas E. Watson. Raised in a fairly comfortable family pushed near poverty by the Civil War and the Panic of 1873, Watson overcame these reverses to become a successful lawyer and state representative by the 1880s. In 1890 the Tenth Congressional District, stretching west from Augusta, chose him as its representative. He championed most of the Alliance

agenda and pushed through the bill that made him the self-professed "father of Rural Free Delivery." Watson broke with the Democrats in 1891 to become a full-fledged Populist. His Atlanta-based *People's Party Paper* was the state's main Populist organ, and with the help of William L. Peek he led many Alliance members into the new political fold. Most of the officeholders who had mouthed support for the Alliance, however, remained with the Democratic establishment.

After the turn of the century, Watson would advance his political career by employing some of the most virulent black-baiting rhetoric Georgia has ever seen, but in the early 1890s he viewed a biracial political coalition of poor farmers as the only mechanism capable of breaking Bourbon dominance.

This Populist challenge so threatened the existing economic order that the Democratic establishment condoned violence, fraud, and economic intimidation to defeat Watson and like-minded candidates. The lack of secret ballots made it possible to buy and retain votes. Despite the Populist appeal, most black ballots apparently went to the Democrats. The established party, in turn, became frightened by the power of the new electorate. Realizing that blacks could de-

termine the balance in struggles between rival white factions, Democrats dedicated themselves to getting rid of Negro voting altogether. By the early twentieth century, the Bourbons had both successfully beaten back the Populist challenge and eliminated the black vote. Again, their undisputed control afforded them the luxury of internal factionalization.

Denied his place in Congress by fraud and intimidation, Watson retreated to his home—called "-Hickory Hill"—near Thomason. He wrote biographies of Andrew Jackson and Thomas Jefferson and penned a popular history of France. He also continued publishing newspapers and magazines. When the People's party endorsed national Democratic presidential nominee William Jennings Bryan in 1896, the Populists tried to maintain a semblance of identity by slating Watson as their vice presidential nominee.

At the close of the century, the New South heralded by many had yet to fully arrive. Georgia boasted more factories than ever before, but she also had more farmers and remained essentially an agricultural state heavily bound to cotton. Meanwhile, the Democrats dominated as a loose coalition of urban, town, and plantation factions.

Right: *These two musicians entertained in southern Georgia at the turn of the century. One played guitar and harmonica simultaneously. Courtesy, Georgia Department of Archives and History*

Facing page: *In 1889 this large family group shared a picnic in Lowndes County. Courtesy, Georgia Department of Archives and History*

Below: *These exotic dancers entertained visitors to Atlanta's Cotton States Exposition in 1895. Courtesy, Atlanta Historical Society*

# 7

## RACE AND REFORM

## IN THE

## NEW CENTURY

*During the late 1920s, the Georgia State Board of Health trained more than 4,000 midwives. Here, one class poses with its instructor. Courtesy, Georgia Department of Archives and History*

This 1916 photo shows workers posed with a Georgia Power Company streetcar in Augusta. Courtesy, Georgia Department of Archives and History

Joel Chandler Harris, a journalist, wrote out the folk tales he had learned from blacks during his childhood in the Georgia plantation belt. These became the beloved Uncle Remus stories. Courtesy, Atlanta Historical Society

The opening decade and a half of the twentieth century is generally called the Progressive Era because of the reform spirit that developed in reaction to social problems accompanying the nation's rapid industrialization and urbanization following the Civil War. Especially in the South, however, conservatism was at least as strong as the urge for change. Yet, the reform that did occur during the Progressive Era in halting ways laid the foundation for Georgia's modern empire. It was an empire, nevertheless, for whites only.

The term "Jim Crow" may have come from a nineteenth-century minstrel tune or may simply have derived from the fact that crows are black. No one knows for sure exactly how the name originated, but there is no doubt about its meaning: in Georgia and the rest of the South, the races were rigidly segregated—more than their ancestors had been in slavery.

The 1910 Georgia census counted 1.43 million whites and 1.18 million blacks, yet the two races did not eat in the same restaurants or sleep in the same inns and hotels. They were assigned different sections of theaters, street cars, and passenger trains. Blacks learned in black schools and worshiped in black churches. Although they often worked side-by-side with whites in homes, businesses, and industry, blacks almost invariably held the menial role of domestic, laborer, porter, or the like. Such was Jim Crow.

The races did not really know each other. Sadly, many Caucasians formed their understanding of Negro culture from the romanticized folk tales rendered in a homey dialect by white journalist Joel Chandler Harris. It is symbolic of Jim Crow that for more than half a century after the writer's death, Negroes could not join the association that honored Harris nor visit his "Wren's Nest" house museum celebrating the tales allegedly told by old black Uncle Remus.

During Reconstruction, Congress had passed laws designed to ensure integrated public accommodations, and in the 1870s there was more racial intermingling than would be accepted later. As white Democrats captured political control, racial attitudes hardened. The United States Supreme Court in 1883 weakened the Fourteenth Amendment's "equal protection" clause by declaring that it did not empower Congress to prohibit private acts of discrimination. Thirteen years later the high court approved

Above: In 1920 some poor, rural Georgians still lived as their ancestors did, in a log cabin with fireplaces and chimneys made of sticks and clay. Courtesy, Georgia Department of Archives and History

Right: Families vacationing in Rabun County liked to pose in front of the Witch's Head rock formation. This group had its picnic there in 1906. Courtesy, Georgia Department of Archives and History

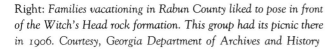

of racial segregation if facilities were "separate but equal."

With no prospect of Northern interference, Georgia and her Southern neighbors began passing laws that would codify and expand Jim Crow customs. The state's earliest such statutes came in 1891 when railroad cars and convict camps were required to be segregated. Black boycotts forced Atlanta and Savannah to back away from trolley car discrimination at first, but by the early 1900s the forces of segregation had triumphed on transit systems throughout the state. Atlanta courts even yielded to the absurdity of requiring black and white witnesses to swear upon separate Bibles.

During Reconstruction and afterward, most white Georgians resented black voting and effectively discouraged many potential Negro electors. Realizing, however, that federal law mandated black enfranchisement, white politicians fought hard for the black ballots, and Bourbon Democrats usually won them. The experience of the 1890s, when Populists and regular Democrats struggled for the potentially influential "swing" faction, convinced the white establishment to try to eliminate black voting altogether.

Mississippi led the southern states in disenfranchisement efforts, but Georgia was not far behind. Although the cumulative poll tax requirement already kept most poor blacks—and many poor whites—from voting, it was not effective enough to satisfy the clamor. The party implemented the primary system of choosing nominees statewide in 1898, and two years later it was officially made a "white primary." Democratic officials evaded the spirit of the Fifteenth Amendment, arguing that since political organizations were private and not state operated, they could set their own rules of membership, excluding blacks. The Republican party never even fielded candidates in most of Georgia, so the Democratic white-only primary proved tantamount to election.

To complete the disenfranchisement movement, voters ratified by a two-to-one margin a constitutional amendment establishing a literacy test (read and interpret a portion of the state or federal constitution) accompanied by a "grandfather clause," a "good character" standard, and a property requirement. Potential voters could avoid the literacy test if they claimed ancestors who had served in the Confederate or Union military forces. Virtually no

Sharecroppers could not afford the luxury of yards or flower gardens. They planted cash crops on every bit of available land, right up to the door of the cabin. Courtesy, Georgia Department of Archives and History

In an address at the Cotton States Exposition in Atlanta, Booker T. Washington, founder of the famed Tuskegee Institute, delineated the Atlanta Doctrine: that hard work and education would be the keys to black success. Courtesy, Atlanta University Center, Woodruff Library, Special Collections and Archives

blacks, of course, could meet such a standard. The "good character" test—later called the "good ol' boy" clause—allowed local registrars to use their own judgment in exempting specific individuals, always white, from the literacy exam. Although a few token black voters remained on the rolls in the cities (mainly Atlanta), the 1908 amendment—combined with earlier efforts—ended meaningful black political participation in Georgia until after the Second World War.

Not only were blacks effectively excluded from politics, they also were kept well outside the mainstream of economic life. Cotton prices rose somewhat after 1900, but Georgia's one-crop agriculture continued to oppress large numbers of both races; blacks suffered more because they were considerably less likely to own their land. Some farmers turned to the factories and cotton mills. Industrial operatives were almost all white, and some people opposed child labor laws because if white youngsters left the mills, black adults might replace them. Similarly, whites nearly monopolized the better paying railroad jobs.

Most urban blacks worked as porters, maids, washwomen, cooks, and the like. For example,

over 63 percent of Atlanta's black workers, but less than five percent of the whites, labored in the domestic and personal service category as of 1910.

Some black city dwellers managed to rise economically through entrepreneurship and the professions. Black preachers, teachers, lawyers, and undertakers were not well paid by white standards, but they did form the core of the black middle class in cities and larger towns. As blacks became more segregated residentially and as they were pushed out of enterprises and trades serving whites, some turned to operating groceries, drugstores, and laundries which could cater to a black clientele. Probably Georgia's most successful black entrepreneur was barber Alonzo F. Herndon, who founded the Atlanta Mutual Life Insurance Company. By the end of 1915 the firm had over one million dollars of insurance in force. Augusta also boasted a black-owned insurance company and a savings bank.

One of the sorriest episodes in Georgia race relations was the Atlanta race riot of 1906. Between 10 and 25 blacks died, and many more were injured as whites moved into black neighborhoods to perpetrate violence. At least one white perished; several

A.F. Herndon began as a barber but built a fortune in the insurance business to become the first important black entrepreneur in Atlanta history. This photo shows "A. F. Herndon's Tonsorial Palace" in the 1903 Souvenir of Atlanta, which highlighted important commercial establishments. Courtesy, Atlanta Historical Society

sustained injuries. The cause remains vague, but the disorder may have grown out of the racial animosity evoked by the gubernatorial primary campaign between Hoke Smith and Clark Howell. The black editor of *Voice of the Negro*, however, blamed the riot on the white newspapers which had printed sensationalized accounts of black attacks on white women. Fearing for his life, the journalist transferred his offices to Chicago.

Blacks also faced violence from lynching. The state's 241 recorded mob actions between 1888 and 1903 only trailed those of Mississippi. Georgia counted 27 such deaths in 1889 alone. The "unmentionable crime"—black rape of white women—provided the most common excuse for lynching, but studies revealed that the majority of episodes did not involve such assaults. Much more often the offense allegedly occurred when a black man attacked a white man. Many of the lynchings were public affairs viewed by large crowds and at least tacitly approved by local authorities.

The major philosophical cleavage among black Americans of the early twentieth century had significant Georgia roots. Booker T. Washington's address at the Cotton States and International Exposition thrust him into leadership of the nation's blacks—at least in the eyes of most whites. "The wisest among my race," Washington reassured white listeners in the mixed crowd, "understand that the agitation of questions of social equality is the extremist folly." With a great open-handed gesture, Washington proclaimed: "In all things that are purely social we can be as separate as the fingers," yet, he went on to say, black and white could pull the fingers together like "the hand in all things essential to mutual progress." If whites would provide fair opportunities for jobs and education in the segregated society, blacks would be "the most patient, faithful, law-abiding, and unresentful people that the world has seen." Governor William Atkinson shook Washington's hand, and the crowd cheered wildly. Editor Clark Howell of the *Atlanta Constitution* judged the speech "a platform upon which blacks and whites can stand with full justice to each other." Washington and black allies such as Benjamin J. Davis, editor of the *Atlanta Independent*, seemed to be saying that "separate but equal" was acceptable to their race. As usual, most whites soon neglected the equality part of the bargain.

Some blacks felt that Washington's "Atlanta

Above: W.E.B. DuBois, a noted scholar and leader in the creation of the National Association for the Advancement of Colored People, taught at Atlanta University from 1897 to 1910, and again from 1933 to 1944. Courtesy, Atlanta University Center, Woodruff Library, Special Collections and Archives

Compromise" gave up too much. Morehouse College President John Hope asked simply, "If we are not striving for equality, in heaven's name for what are we living?" In the *Georgia Baptist*, Augusta editor William J. White urged his fellow blacks to actively protest.

Most notable among Washington's critics was W.E.B. DuBois, a professor at Atlanta University from 1897 to 1909. His academic work was in sociology and included an impressive study of landowning among Georgia blacks. DuBois was a principal founder of the National Association for the Advancement of Colored People, and in 1910 he left Atlanta to edit the NAACP's *Crisis*.

Besides the ever-present racial difficulties, Georgians looked for answers to old problems like too much alcohol and too little education; corporate arrogance and exploited labor; and an abusive criminal justice system and corruptible politicians. Progressivism in Georgia sputtered and coughed, offering nothing but further restrictions for blacks. Yet, positive accomplishments came about.

Georgia's leading progressive was Hoke Smith. Born in North Carolina, he came to Georgia as a teenager when his father accepted a position with the

Atlanta public schools. Young Smith began his legal practice with an unsuccessful stint as an Atlanta attorney. But his talent for the law was rewarding enough that in 1887, at age 32, he purchased controlling interest in the *Atlanta Journal*. His paper soon challenged the *Constitution* in circulation, and Smith made a handsome profit when he sold his interest in 1900. He used the *Journal* and his wide connections to boost Grover Cleveland's successful bid to return to the presidency; the New Yorker subsequently showed his gratitude by making Smith the new Secretary of Interior.

In June 1905, more than one year before the primary, Smith began an ambitious campaign for governor. The 25,000 miles of travel paid off when he handily defeated four opponents, most notably Clark Howell, former speaker of the state house of representatives, member of the Georgia Senate, protege of Henry Grady, editor of the *Atlanta Constitution*, and generally a bitter and longtime rival.

Hoke Smith favored many reforms. He vigorously attacked railroads and called for public school improvement. Yet the centerpiece of his campaign was a strident call for white supremacy and more complete black disenfranchisement. In this crusade Smith

Above: *These revenue agents prepare to destroy a moonshine still in 1900. Courtesy, Georgia Department of Archives and History*

Left: *These convict laborers were photographed on Walton Way Plantation, near Augusta, in 1900. Courtesy, Georgia Department of Archives and History*

joined hands with Tom Watson, who had several years earlier abandoned his ideas of racial cooperation and had become, in contrast, an apostle of venomous hatred.

Newly elected Governor Hoke Smith set out to fulfill his promises. In addition to disenfranchisement, the state saw legislative action on railroad regulation, penal reform, prohibition, and public school improvement.

The post-Civil War railroad boom demanded cheap labor to lay what seemed to be endless track. Over the years many prominent Georgians—including Joseph E. Brown, John B. Gordon, and James Monroe Smith (probably the state's largest planter)—leased convicts. Stories abounded of mistreatment of men and sexual abuse of women prisoners, and several legislative investigations unearthed scandal. But the system continued because it saved money for both the lessee, who rented convicts for less than the going wage rate, and for the state and counties, which did not have to maintain large institutions to house prisoners.

Three southern states abolished their leasing plans in the 1890s, while Georgia moderated its system a bit by establishing a prison farm for women,

youth, and the infirm. Not until 1908, however, did public outcry over mistreatment and financial mismanagement finally bring an end to this virtual slave-labor practice. As one member of the General Assembly said, "the convict lease system is so rotten that it smells to heaven."

The cure, ironically, proved nearly as bad as the disease. In place of private convict leasing with limited supervision, the new law allowed state and county governments to use prisoners for road improvements—a special need with the advent of the automobile. Public chain-gang conditions in some jurisdictions were just as brutal as they had been under the lease system.

Local governments gained increasing control of administrative functions, too. As early as 1885 Georgia had permitted individual counties to ban the use of alcohol, and most of them had done so by 1906. On the other hand, many counties, including the large urban ones such as Fulton (Atlanta), Richmond (Augusta), Bibb (Macon), Chatham (Savannah), Muscogee (Columbus), and Floyd (Rome) remained "wet." Labeling these areas "foul blots," the Woman's Christian Temperance Union implored, "We'll sing them out and pray them out and

educate them out, We'll talk them out and vote them out and legislate them out." And they did! Charges that intoxicated blacks had inflamed the Atlanta race riot helped push a statewide prohibition bill in 1907.

One of the most effective prohibitionists was Rebecca Latimer Felton. Her career began when she organized her husband's political campaigns as an independent Democratic congressman in the 1870s. She also developed a large following through the Cartersville paper and *Atlanta Journal* columns which she wrote for over 20 years. An early feminist and women's suffragette, she was a principal leader in the struggles against convict leasing and liquor. Felton proved victorious in the latter crusades, but she saw her state defiantly reject the Nineteenth Amendment granting voting rights to women. (Georgia finally and symbolically ratified the amendment in 1970, 50 years after women became part of the electorate.) On other issues, including race and lynching, Felton appeared as profoundly reactionary as Tom Watson, whom she greatly admired. Even her prescription for the advancement of women offered no challenge to the social order of town, mill village, or farm.

Educational improvement was also a major plank of the progressive agenda in Georgia and the South. First authorized by the 1868 constitution, a racially segregated system of public education gradually developed in the 1870s and 1880s under the leadership of Gustavus J. Orr. The constitution of 1877 then confined state allocations to elementary schools and colleges only. Therefore, secondary education be-

Above: *The backfield of the Mary Persons High School football team posed for this 1931 photograph, which included Dan Driskell, Robert Abernathy, Joe Dorner, and Dick Writs. Courtesy, Georgia Department of Archives and History*

Facing page, top: *Margaret Koch drove this automobile float for the Young People's Suffrage Association. Courtesy, Georgia Department of Archives and History*

Below: *John Hope, seated, president of Morehouse College, signs the 1929 affiliation agreement creating the Atlanta University Center, whereby Atlanta's black colleges joined to share resources. Looking on are president Florence M. Read of Spelman College and the president of Atlanta University, Myron W. Adams. Courtesy, Atlanta University Center, Woodruff Library, Special Collections and Archives*

came the responsibility of local governments. As would continue to be the case for more than a century, city schools maintained a more extensive curriculum and much better funding base than those in the rural areas. The worst schools of all were those provided for blacks in the old plantation belt. Wide funding disparities between white and black schools characterized the system from the beginning, and Progressive Era reforms did nothing to remedy the imbalance.

In 1903 the whole state had only a dozen full-fledged high schools, graduating a mere 600 students. With guidance from the University of Georgia, accreditation standards for secondary-level institutions were developed. A major push for state-funded high schools emerged, and the school commissioner tried to gain business support for this endeavor, declaring: "It is an economic measure, and will bring back financial returns." Finally, in 1912 a constitutional amendment overturned the 1877 prohibition on state tax support for secondary schools. Georgia thus became the last state in the union to incorporate free public high schools into its educational system. By 1920 the state claimed 169 accredited white high schools.

Higher learning also developed during the early twentieth century. The Morrill Land Grant Act provided federal funds to the University of Georgia from 1872 for agricultural and mechanical education. Branch agricultural schools were established at Dahlonega and elsewhere, and federal money for Negro education went exclusively to Atlanta University until government pressure resulted in the 1890 founding of the institution that would become Savannah State College.

Besides Atlanta University, blacks were educated at other church-supported private institutions, including Morehouse (1867), Clark (1870), Spelman (1881), Morris Brown (1881) in Atlanta, and Paine College (1881) in Augusta. A second state college for blacks was set up in Albany in 1917.

Macon's Methodist-sponsored Wesleyan College had been serving young white ladies since 1836, and in 1889 the state began providing higher educa-

tion for females at the Georgia Normal and Industrial School in Milledgeville. Georgia lagged behind its neighbors in coeducation. No women attended the University of Georgia until the summer session of 1903, and it would be 15 more years before females could be admitted as regular students.

Among the many changes that developed after the turn of the century, probably the most notable was the University of Georgia's progress toward becoming a true university rather than a tiny liberal arts college. State funding increased, the physical plant expanded greatly, enrollment rose, and new schools and departments were organized.

In 1904 a delegation of Georgia leaders traveled to the University of Wisconsin at Madison to observe the workings of a fine state school. Two years later, the legislature appropriated $100,000 to start an agricultural and mechanical college. Between 1908 and 1917 the university established a small graduate program and schools of commerce, education, and journalism. From 38 faculty and 383 students in 1900, the figures climbed to 137 faculty and 1,664 students within twenty years.

Destined to become the state's leading private institution, Emory was organized as a university in

Atlanta in 1915 by the Southern Methodists, with generous help from Coca-Cola founder Asa Griggs Candler and the Atlanta Chamber of Commerce. The former Oxford campus, dating from 1838, became a junior college. About the same time, the Atlanta area also captured the reorganized Oglethorpe University, which had operated near Milledgeville before and shortly after the Civil War. Baptist-supported Mercer University in Macon survived the national upheaval as a small but well-established institution, and the state was sprinkled with several other small, denominational colleges. An educational effort which attracted national support began in 1902, when Martha Berry started a school near Rome for poor children of the Blue Ridge. By the end of the 1920s, Berry was offering college-level work.

Georgia stepped into the twentieth century with a weak and spotty state-supported elementary education system and a few shoestring colleges. As World War I ended and the state entered the 1920s, something resembling a coherent system of public schools and colleges emerged. Yet Georgia education still lagged behind the nation and region despite its apparent progress.

Facing page: When this Rabun County family posed for a turn-of-the-century photographer they included their most prized possessions: the family Bible, an accordion, and a pair of handsome draft animals. Courtesy, Georgia Department of Archives and History

Below: In 1912 members of the Baptist Tabernacle of Shellnut Creek gathered for an outdoor baptism. The minister, shown in the foreground, has a white cloth over his left shoulder. Courtesy, Georgia Department of Archives and History

# 8

## GROWING CITIES,

## CHANGING

## COUNTRYSIDE,

## AND TOUGH TIMES

*These participants in the 1935 harvest festival display grapes grown on the cooperative farm created by the Works Progress Administration at Pine Mountain, Georgia. Courtesy, Atlanta Historical Society*

From the prosperity of World War I to the slump of 1920-1921, and from the boom of the Roaring Twenties to the stock market crash of 1929 and the ensuing decade of depression, the country's economy was on a roller coaster ride. Georgia's version of this ride, however, contained less lofty highs and ominously deeper lows than the nation as a whole. The cities—especially Atlanta—expanded in size, business, and culture during the 1920s, only to face grave crisis during the next decade. In the meantime, Georgia farmers reeled from blow to blow through the early 1920s, recovering only slightly before being devastated by the Depression.

Using a population of 2,500 to designate urban areas, the United States census of 1920 was the first to show that a majority of Americans lived in cities. Yet the South, including Georgia, remained mostly rural until after World War II. The trends that would make Georgia an urban and metropolitan state were already in place by 1920, however. On the eve of the Civil War only 7 percent of all its citizens lived in urban areas—compared to the national rate of 20 percent; by 1920 Georgia's percentage had more than tripled to 25, about half the national percentage. Whites were slightly more urbanized than blacks.

Throughout this period, Georgia's portion of city dwellers almost exactly matched that of the South as a whole.

The state's urban population, in fact, had grown relatively faster than rural population in every decade since 1810, but it took 150 years to redress the 98:2 rural-urban ratio of the early-nineteenth century. The rural count showed an absolute increase every 10 years up to 1920, even though the cities grew faster. Then in the 1920s a historic turning point occurred: for the first time Georgia's rural population actually declined. The 7.1 percent drop was temporarily reversed by the "back to the land" movement of the Depression decade, with its tiny 1.8 percent absolute increase in rural population. But the 1940s and 1950s returned to the previous pattern of rural decline.

A combination of push and pull factors caused the turnaround. Agricultural distress jolted marginal farmers off the land, while new urban opportunities attracted people. Most farms did not have telephones or electricity, but both were commonplace for the middle class and the more prosperous portion of urban workers. The cities' magnetism also included motion pictures, stage shows, and radios. WSB, "the

Above: *American millionaires made Dungeness, on Cumberland Island, a playground. Courtesy, Georgia Department of Archives and History*

Right: *In 1920, Douglass Davis was considered a Georgia aviation pioneer. Courtesy, Atlanta Historical Society*

voice of the South," began its Atlanta-based broadcasts in 1922. The first major Southern airmail route went through Atlanta's Candler Field in 1926, and by 1930 Eastern Air Transport offered passenger service to New York, portending the Gate City's rise as an aviation hub as well as a railroad and highway center.

Urban growth between 1900 and 1940 was impressive in all five of Georgia's major cities and their surrounding counties. Bibb County (Macon) entered the century at 50,493 and had nearly doubled its population four decades later. Metropolitan Augusta claimed 53,735 in 1900 and 131,779 in 1940, with the census bureau including some nearby South Carolinians in the latter figure. Columbus also became a two-state metropolis by 1940. Thanks in large part to the World War I and pre-World War II military buildup at Fort Benning, the Chattahoochee textile capital and its environs boasted 126,407 residents in 1940, almost 100,000 more than Muscogee County had had 40 years earlier. Growth in Georgia's earliest city was slower, but Savannah also forged ahead, going from just over 71,000 to almost 118,000.

Atlanta stood out most, however. Within 15 years of Appomattox, the piedmont transportation hub had passed Savannah as Georgia's largest city. A writer for *Harper's New Monthly Magazine* observed this historic shift in 1879 and explained the reasons for it:

*How, then, did Atlanta come to exist at all; and much more, how did she succeed like the goddess whose name she suggests, in outstripping all her older sisters, Augusta, Savannah, Macon, and the rest? The answer is found in one word—railways . . . So deriving her success from a multitude of business advantages, and from her favorable situation in point of geography and climate, Atlanta has waxed great and powerful.*

From its fifth-place status among Southern cities in 1880, Atlanta rose to fourth in 1890 and third in 1900. The Gate City had passed Richmond, Nashville, Charleston, and Mobile, as well as Savannah, in its climb from 1870. New Orleans remained the largest southern metropolis until after World War II. Reviving the best tradition of Henry Grady, Atlanta boosters launched a "Forward Atlanta" campaign in the mid-1920s to attract business and industry to the city. The effort cost nearly one million dollars, but its leaders, including chairman Ivan Allen,

On May 21, 1917, fire swept across 300 acres of Atlanta, destroying nearly 2,000 houses and leaving 10,000 persons homeless. Firefighters found it necessary to dynamite rows of houses in order to create a firebreak and stop the relentless flames. Courtesy, Atlanta Historical Society

claimed that 20,000 jobs had been created.

The automobile became crucial to Atlanta and other Georgia cities. Atlanta first required automobile registration in 1904-1905, and only 99 cars were recorded. Fifteen years later, the capital city claimed 80 automobile dealers and Savannah 33. Vehicles so jammed Broad Street in downtown Augusta on Saturdays that traffic nearly came to a standstill despite the efforts of several policemen. As late as 1922 the president of Atlanta's streetcar company professed not to fear competition from the new invention because, in his words, "the great majority of people will never be able to afford the ownership of an automobile." Yet, by 1930 over 60,000 motor vehicles were registered in Fulton County.

Federal funds for highway construction became available in 1916, and the state soon established a commission and a building program. Georgia's traditional low-tax parsimony, however, limited construction. The dollar value of convict chain-gang labor was often used for the required local matching. Rural roads not eligible for federal dollars received very little attention, and most farm-to-market routes remained dirt until after World War II. Still, Georgia had about 13,000 miles of state highways and a half-million vehicles by 1940.

Railroad mileage in the state peaked around World War I at roughly 7,500. Although trains like the Nancy Hanks from Atlanta to Savannah would continue to carry passengers for many more years, competition from cars and trucks after 1920 resulted in a slow but steady abandonment of track.

As early as 1903 talk focused on the development of a great highway that would connect the Midwest with the heart of the South. The governors of Georgia, Florida, and Tennessee met with their colleagues from Illinois, Indiana, and Ohio in 1915 to map out a route for what would be dubbed "The Dixie Highway." In November 1929 a cavalcade of 200 cars left Atlanta on the recently completed highway. Townspeople in Marietta, Calhoun, Cartersville, and Dalton cheered as the procession headed toward a grand celebration at the summit of Lookout Mountain above Chattanooga and the Tennessee River. The automobile route chosen never strayed more than a few miles from the tracks that the W & A had laid some 90 years before.

As the Dixie Highway neared completion, a series of viaducts covered the jumbled railroad tracks which had rendered vehicle access to downtown

Right, top: *Streetcars and auto-mobiles competed for space on Atlanta's South Broad Street in 1926. Courtesy, Atlanta Historical Society*

Right, bottom: *For more than half a century the Tallulah Falls Railroad carried passengers over this trestle on the 58-mile trip between Cornelia, Georgia, and Franklin, North Carolina. This photo was taken in 1907. Courtesy, Georgia Department of Archives and History*

Atlanta difficult. Massive concrete structures isolated the former street levels of dozens of buildings into a dank underground. The W & A had been paralleled by highways in the mountains and covered by streets in the city—Georgia's future was on rubber tires.

By the end of the 1920s, for the first time in Georgia history, the majority of citizens worked in non-agricultural jobs. Retail and trade employment particularly flourished. Industrial growth was steady but not spectacular.

One great Georgia business went through an important transition in the post-World War I decade. Dr. John Pemberton developed Coca-Cola in his Atlanta laboratory during the 1880s. At the end of the decade, Pemberton sold out to a group that included Asa Griggs Candler, and by 1895 the new soft drink was being sold in every state. Under the guidance of Candler, the Coca-Cola emblem became a common sight, as it decorated trays, clocks, glasses, and signs all across America. The company's advertising budget exceeded one million dollars by 1912.

In 1919 the Candler family sold Coca-Cola for $25 million to a syndicate put together by Ernest Woodruff, president of the Trust Company of Geor-

Above: *Asa G. Candler bought the patent for the Coca-Cola formula and began merchandising it as a "delicious and refreshing" drink. This laid the groundwork for the corporation that he served as president from 1892 to 1916. After retiring from this position, he served as mayor of Atlanta. He developed the Druid Hills neighborhood, hiring the design firm of Frederick Law Olmstead to plan it, and gave an adjoining tract of land for the new campus of Emory University. Courtesy, Coca-Cola Company*

Right: *This photograph from the archives of the Coca-Cola Company depicts the Coca-Cola headquarters organization in 1899. Courtesy, Coca-Cola Company*

gia. Four years later, Woodruff's son, Robert, assumed command of the Coca-Cola empire. The company was on its way to world dominance in the soft drink industry. Both the Candlers and Woodruffs have given millions of dollars over the years to worthy Atlanta causes, especially Emory University. Ironically, Columbus, the home of much smaller Royal Crown Cola, is part of the Coke story. Pemberton practiced medicine there before moving to Atlanta in 1870, and Ernest Woodruff was born in Columbus during the Civil War.

Georgia's cities and larger towns indeed offered opportunities for business prosperity, education, and high culture not available to the rural folk, but tragically the same metropolitan areas also provoked intolerance. The racial climate in Georgia's capital had been especially tense since the 1906 riot and the controversy surrounding the disenfranchisement amendments of 1908. The 1915 case of Jewish factory manager Leo Frank stirred up anti-semitism to accompany the pervasive racism. Frank was convicted of slaying a young working girl. Although the conviction held up on appeal, enough doubt about the case existed so that Governor John M. Slaton commuted the death sentence to life imprisonment. An

angry mob snatched Frank from prison and lynched him in Marietta, the girl's home town. National Guard troops had to be called out to protect Governor Slaton from throngs angry at his action. Meanwhile, America's entry into World War I agitated extreme nationalism, and after the fighting a wave of anti-alien, anti-radical sentiment swept the nation. Ex-Populist Tom Watson constantly encouraged racism, denouncing Jews, Catholics, and blacks in his speeches and writings. On the other hand, Watson opposed the patriotic excesses that accompanied World War I.

Out of this cauldron of racism, anti-semitism, and xenophobia, the new Klan emerged in 1915. The motion picture *Birth of a Nation* glorified the Reconstruction-era organization, and Alabaman William J. Simmons timed his resurrection of the Klan with the film's Atlanta opening. On Thanksgiving eve a small group of men climbed Stone Mountain east of Atlanta and ceremoniously burned a cross at a crude stone altar—the new Ku Klux Klan was born. Only "one hundred percent American" white Protestants could join the local lodges, and the organization embraced thousands, including many politicians. An Atlanta company became the official maker

of Klan regalia; the Invisible Empire also chose the Georgia Savings Building as its first headquarters.

The Klan briefly held state political power. Governor Thomas W. Hardwick tried to appease the group with kind words, but when he proposed an unmasking law, the Klan helped beat him for reelection. The victor, Clifford Walker, was an admitted Klan member, who spoke at meetings of the order.

Klan opposition came mainly from newspaper editors, most notably Julian Harris of the *Columbus Enquirer-Sun.* Son of Uncle Remus creator Joel Chandler Harris, the journalist resisted threats of violence to continue his Pulitzer Prize-winning crusade. He once even referred to Georgia as "the Empire State of Illiteracy."

Internal dissension racked the Klan, however, and many white citizens felt revulsion at violent incidents. The feelings of prejudice that the Klan exploited did not disappear, but by 1926 the organized Invisible Empire was on the decline in Georgia. National headquarters moved to Washington, D.C., and Klan-backed candidates did poorly at the polls.

During World War I, Southern farmers were riding high. The fighting stimulated demand for cotton and prices rose impressively. Soon, however, two suc- cessive blows hit staple agriculture: prices for all commodities dropped precipitously after peace arrived, and the boll weevil, which had been creeping eastward from Texas since the 1890s, began devastating Georgia fields.

The 1918 cotton crop surpassed two million bales and sold for 28 cents per pound. The next year, production dropped to 1.66 million bales, but the price rose to 36 cents. Then the bottom dropped out as prices stayed between 15 and 17 cents in 1920-1921.

Meanwhile, boll weevil larvae destroyed crops in many counties. In Morgan County, about midway between Augusta and Atlanta, the 1920 production of 7,000 bales was one-fifth the 1919 figure. Adjacent Green County's 362-bale output (1920) barely came to one-sixth of the previous year's output. Statewide, the drop was from a 2.1-million-bale record in 1918 to a .59-million-bale disaster in 1923. The state commissioner of agriculture declared that he had never seen the farm economy "so depressed and in such an alarming financial condition." Drought and insecticide gradually controlled the infestation, and within a couple of years the crop reached one million bales again. Yet the crown of King Cotton was forever tar-

Laborers moved cotton in and out of Strickland's Cotton Warehouse in Carrollton, Georgia, in 1930. Courtesy, Georgia Department of Archives and History

nished. In 1920 the fluffy white staple accounted for 66 percent of Georgia's farm value. Ten years later it had tumbled to half, and by 1940 it stood at merely 40 percent. As the cotton fields moved west to Arkansas, Oklahoma, and Texas, peanuts, pecans, soybeans, and livestock made gains in Georgia. For a while the state trailed only California in its peach crop, but low prices cut output significantly.

Less cotton also meant fewer tenants, and Negro sharecroppers almost immediately began their exodus. In fact, Georgia's principal export during the 1920s was black people. Natural increase proved insufficient to replace the thousands who migrated north, and Georgia had 135,440 fewer blacks by the end of the decade—an 11.2 percent decline. *Tenants of the Almighty*, a famous sociological account of Greene County, spoke of this phenomenon. "They were usually headed for distant cities—Birmingham or Detroit, Chicago or Philadelphia, Cincinnati or Washington—to look for work. But most of them stopped in Atlanta or Athens or Augusta, for they had no money to go farther." Many, of course, eventually did go farther. Although it did not promise abundant riches or an absence of prejudice, the North did offer more jobs and fewer racial barriers.

For Georgians—both black and white—the twenties had not roared with the same prosperity as they had in the rest of the nation. The advent of the Great Depression, therefore, simply meant going from bad to worse. Farm prices dropped an average of 60 percent from 1929 to 1932. Cotton plummeted to a nickel per pound. Not since the depression of the mid-1890s had prices fallen so low.

With the release of Erskine Caldwell's 1932 novel, much of the nation came to regard Georgia as one long *Tobacco Road*. Indeed, the novel focused on "the story of the landless and poverty-stricken families living on East Georgia sand hills and tobacco roads." The author later recalled, "I wanted to tell the story of the people I knew in the manner in which they actually lived . . . Families on tenant farms were huddled around fireplaces in drafty hovels. Most of them were despondent." Many Georgians confronted the frank portrayals in the book and play with anger and shock. In 1937 Caldwell and photographer Margaret Bourke-White together produced *You Have Seen Their Faces*, a collection of images and text which demonstrated the essential accuracy of the writer's fictional accounts.

President Franklin D. Roosevelt addressed real-

Above: *Residents of the New Deal's cooperative farm in 1935 at Pine Mountain, Georgia, took pride in their handsome livestock. Courtesy, Atlanta Historical Society*

Left: *Franklin Delano Roosevelt, himself a victim of the disease, founded a therapy center for polio victims at Warm Springs, Georgia. He visited there often during his Presidency. He died at his Little White House nearby in 1945. Courtesy, Atlanta Historical Society*

Below: *Governor Eurith Dickinson Rivers spoke to his constituents in Suches, Union County, in April 1939, while WSB radio broadcast the speech. Courtesy, Georgia Department of Archives and History*

ity when he commissioned a study of economic conditions in the South, describing the region as "the Nation's No. 1 economic problem—the Nation's problem, not merely the South's." Roosevelt, of course, spoke partly from personal observation, for since 1924 he had been traveling to Warm Springs for relaxation and polio therapy. Part of the surrounding Pine Mountain area later became a demonstration project for New Deal ideas about rural community development. A large Civilian Conservation Corps camp also was established nearby.

In Georgia, as in the rest of the nation, the Depression's urgency and Roosevelt's personality and programs dominated politics. The best known public figure in Georgia during the 1930s and 1940s, however, was an outspoken critic of the president. Born into a fairly affluent south Georgia family, Eugene Talmadge pursued both law and farming, though he failed to attain more than moderate success at either. His real talent proved to be in the political arena. Although a third-generation college man, Talmadge convinced voters that he was just a plain dirt farmer. He served three terms as Commissioner of Agriculture, then ran a colorful and successful campaign for governor in 1932 telling one audience, "You farmers

haven't had anybody fight for you since Tom Watson." Capturing the executive office, he reduced ad valorem taxes, set car license tag fees at three dollars, and got utility rates lowered. He used high-handed tactics to accomplish his goals, and big businesses may have benefited more than the common people. Yet, the voters loved him.

Talmadge thwarted cooperation with many New Deal programs, and so frustrated Roosevelt that Georgia turned out to be one of the few states in which the national government federalized welfare. Ineligible to run for another term in 1936, Talmadge challenged United States Senator Richard Russell and was beaten badly. At the same time Speaker of the House E.D. Rivers, a New Deal supporter, won the gubernatorial election over a Talmadge protege. Rivers journeyed to Washington to find out what Georgia needed to do to cooperate, and he proceeded to issue executive orders and request legislation launching a "Little New Deal." The large state deficit, controversy over several dozen last-minute pardons, and allegations of corruption tainted the Rivers' memory despite his accomplishments.

New Deal agricultural policy profoundly affected Georgia farms, accentuating the outmigration of tenants and further lessening dependence on cotton. The central goal of the Agricultural Adjustment Act was to raise prices by reducing production of basic commodities—including cotton and tobacco. During the 1930s the number of sharecroppers in Georgia dropped by 40,000, divided about evenly between blacks and whites. The New Deal also helped meet the needs of veteran city dwellers, as well as the newcomers who drifted in from the depressed countryside. Gay B. Shepperson, who administered several of Georgia's New Deal programs including the Works Progress Administration, distributed relief despite Governor Talmadge's obstructionist efforts. The initiative of businessman Charles F. Palmer introduced Atlanta to the nation's first public housing/slum clearance projects. Techwood Homes was erected for whites and University Homes for blacks. Several other Georgia cities also built public housing projects with New Deal dollars.

Talmadge once again ran for the U.S. Senate in 1938, and as had been the case two years earlier, he vigorously attacked the New Deal. The seasoned campaigner criticized incumbent Senator Walter F. George for being too supportive of Roosevelt, but when FDR turned around and charged that George had been an impediment to him, the Talmadge barrage lost its sting; George handily won reelection. Governor Rivers narrowly retained his position, but he faced a hostile General Assembly that refused him

a tax increase.

Throughout the Depression, the Atlanta-based Commission on Interracial Cooperation worked to ensure the fair administration of relief efforts. Founded in 1919 and vilified by many whites for its liberal, pro-black stance, the CIC essentially remained conservative inasmuch as it accepted the basic premise of Jim Crow while fighting for a separation that was truly equal.

As the decade closed, many CIC members had begun to see that a true racial solution would require the end of Jim Crow rather than accommodation to it. By 1944 the organization had evolved into the Southern Regional Council, which would play a major role in the upcoming civil rights revolution.

Perhaps the rural doldrums of the 1920s and the economic disruptions of the 1930s proved to be a blessing in disguise for the Empire State of the South. Until the chains of one-crop, tenant-based agriculture were broken, Georgia could not modernize and flourish economically. It is often said that while the New Deal may have ended the Depression, it took World War II to restore prosperity. In Georgia, though, the Depression quashed the old order and the war ushered in the new.

Right: *Georgia Governor Eugene Talmadge possessed a spellbinding oratorical style. Courtesy, Georgia Department of Archives and History*

Facing page: *The Works Progress Administration of Franklin Delano Roosevelt's New Deal brought jobs and improvements to Georgia. These large pipes were part of a drainage project. Courtesy, Atlanta Historical Society*

Below: *Seven former governors of Georgia posed together in 1939, including E.D. Rivers, Eugene Talmadge, Richard B. Russell, Clifford M. Walker, Thomas W. Hardwick, Hugh M. Dorsey, and John M. Slaton. Courtesy, Atlanta Historical Society*

# 9

## STRUGGLING TO JOIN

## THE MAINSTREAM

*The Augusta Masters' tournament attracts crowds each year. Courtesy, Georgia Department of Archives and History*

Left: *Georgians enjoy celebrating special occasions with a barbecue. The Savannah Sugar Refinery celebrated its thirtieth anniversary in 1947 with a barbecue for its employees. Courtesy, Georgia Department of Archives and History*

Facing page: *Peaches have been a commercial crop in Georgia since the 1870s. This photograph, dated 1944, shows peach packers filling crates for shipment. Courtesy, Georgia Department of Archives and History*

At the end of the 1930s, the South remained the nation's number one economic problem, and Georgia still languished in depression. But over the next three decades the state made great strides in overcoming its two greatest problems: a lackluster agricultural sector still heavily tied to cotton, and persistent racism that confined 33 percent of the population to second-class status.

Almost one-third of a million Georgians served in the armed forces in World War II, and nearly 7,000 of them died. Impressed by such patriotic valor and believing that if a man was old enough to fight, he should be old enough to cast his ballot, Georgia became the first state to lower its voting age to 18.

During the war, everyday folks saved scrap iron, staffed USO centers, and participated in blackout drills, while chafing under gasoline and rubber rationing. Celebrities such as Margaret Mitchell, author of *Gone With the Wind*, lent their prestige to war bond drives and other projects. Mitchell had the unique opportunity of christening two cruisers named *Atlanta* (the first was sunk in the Pacific in 1942).

The massive influx of federal dollars proved a significant turning point for the Empire State and the rest of the South. When planners in Washington were deciding what military facilities to expand and where to locate new sites, they looked for places that could offer good weather and influential politicians. Georgia had both, and the state's combination of climate and clout served it well. Only Texas exceeded Georgia in the number of wartime training facilities.

All of Georgia's big cities and several smaller towns boasted large installations. The most significant were at the Columbus site of Fort Benning, which bustled with infantry; Warner Robins Air Field, near Macon, where 15,000 civilians obtained employment; Camp Gordon on the west edge of Augusta; and Fort Stewart and Hunter Army Air Field at Savannah. Smaller operations included an airfield at Valdosta which later became Moody Air Force Base, and the Glynco Naval Air Station near Brunswick, a base for blimps patrolling the southern Atlantic coast in search of German submarines. British air cadets trained at Souther Field in Americus, and German prisoners were held at Augusta, Americus, and several other cities.

A ring of military facilities encircled Atlanta. To the northeast a naval air station and military hospital operated on a World War I site in the Chamblee area.

The southwest part of the city housed old Fort McPherson, which found new life as a major induction center. In Clayton County to the southeast the army constructed huge storage facilities and a railroad yard for the Atlanta General Depot.

Most impressive of the Atlanta-based military installations was the massive Bell Bomber plant in Marietta about 20 miles northwest of downtown. This factory began turning out B-29s in September 1943, employing as many as 30,000 men and women.

Military contracts boosted industry across the state. The Chevrolet plant in south Atlanta converted to war production as did several textile mills. Macon and Milledgeville boasted ordnance plants. The Augusta Arsenal employed 1,800 workers to manufacture bombsights and related items. Savannah's flourishing shipyard constructed several minesweepers and 88 cargo-carrying Liberty ships. The yard engaged 15,000 people, including 3,500 women, at its height of operations.

The warm southern states as a whole received more military posts than their northern counterparts. Georgia got her fair share and more for three very significant reasons: Senator Richard B. Russell, Jr., Senator Walter F. George, and Representative Carl Vinson. A senator since 1932, Russell served on the Appropriations and Naval Affairs committees. George, who came to the Senate a decade before Russell, sat on the Foreign Affairs Committee and chaired the tax-writing Finance Committee throughout the war.

Representative Vinson was even more influential in military matters than his Senate colleagues. Elected in 1914, he had been an advocate of preparedness prior to World War I. He chaired the Naval Affairs Committee from 1931, and used his position to deter strong isolationist sentiment. Becoming the driving force behind a significant naval buildup, Vinson and his allies also ensured the construction of such ships as the 10,000-ton cruiser *Savannah*, launched in 1938. "I do not know where this country would have been after December 7, 1941," Admiral Chester Nimitz proclaimed, "if it had not had the ships . . . for which one Vinson bill after another was responsible."

Economic adjustments after the war were inevitable, but Georgia and the nation escaped the depression that many observers had predicted. Pent-up demand for housing, automobiles, and other consumer items fueled the economy. In metropolitan Atlanta

*In 1940 workers carried hand-picked cotton to the scales for weighing. Today, mechanization has ended this traditional method of harvesting. Courtesy, Georgia Department of Archives and History*

the Bell Bomber plant closed, but by the end of the 1940s Ford and General Motors had opened major new assembly plants to the south and north of the city, respectively. With many smaller facilities ceasing operation, the major military installations near Columbus, Macon, Augusta, and Savannah nevertheless remained. Several army airfields, including Daniel in Augusta and Travis in Savannah, were converted for civilian use.

With the onset of the Korean War in 1950, military facilities flourished all around the state. The Bell plant reopened as Lockheed-Georgia. This 76-acre factory, the largest industrial facility under one roof in the country, produced 394 medium-weight B-47 jet bombers before switching to the C-130 Hercules transports that were to become its mainstay.

Like New Deal farm programs, the war forced significant change on Georgia agriculture. Wartime demand brought higher prices for cotton and incentives to move into other commodities. To meet the demand for crops rich in vegetable oil, the government encouraged the planting of peanuts. By 1942 Georgia led the nation in goober production. Government goals also encouraged Georgians to cultivate livestock, and the piedmont area southeast of Atlanta became an important dairy region. Truck farming also flourished.

Thousands of young Georgians left farms and farming communities to enter the armed forces or to take war-related jobs in the cities. The number of tenants, which had begun to decline in the 1930s, further shrank. Black tenants not only vacated their jobs, but the region as well, because racial discrimination severely limited their opportunities in the southern war industry. During the war and after, country shacks were abandoned.

Annual per capita net income for southern farmers leapt from $150 in 1940 to $454 in 1944. Though still lagging behind the $530 national average, the gap was narrowing.

The presence of a tractor became the mark of a modern farm, and those who could afford one (about $1,250 in 1945) were generally the more efficient producers with larger acreage. A 1949 study by the Georgia Agricultural Experiment Station found that farms with tractors planted less cotton and corn, and put more effort into grains and livestock. In 1940 there were only 10,000 tractors in the entire state; by the mid-1950s the number had grown to over 80,000. Not until the 1960s was the majority of the cotton

crop harvested mechanically. By that time, however, the center of cotton cultivation had moved west of the Mississippi River; the day of King Cotton in Georgia was finally over.

The emergence of commercial poultry production caused another important change in Georgia agriculture. The father of the state's poultry industry was Jess Dixon Jewell, a Gainesville feed dealer. Beginning in 1936 he began selling chicks and feed to farmers, while marketing the mature broilers. Over 7,000 commercial poultry farms flourished in the state by 1950—second only to Texas.

Modernization had fully arrived by the mid-1970s, when virtually every measure of Georgia farming proved markedly different than it had been at the end of World War II. Broilers led in farm production, followed by peanuts, eggs, cattle, and hogs. Soybeans and feed grains were also important. As of 1950, tenants operated 43 percent of Georgia's farm units, but 25 years later the figure had declined to under 8 percent. There were nearly 200,000 farms in the state at mid-century; only about 60,000 survived a generation later. The average Georgia grower harvested 36 acres in 1950 and 111 in 1978. Finally, those wedded to the soil numbered 962,000 during the 1950 census, but there were fewer than 200,000 by the time a Georgia peanut farmer sat in the White House.

Political changes appeared as dramatic as economic ones. In 1940 former Governor Gene Talmadge seemed, according to his biographer William Anderson, "confident" and "mellow." Having been twice chastened by voters who refused to send him to the United States Senate, "the wild man from Sugar Creek" moderated his anti-Roosevelt stance and adopted a fairly progressive program. A "giant rushing wave" of support returned the new Talmadge to the governor's mansion.

The temporarily tame Talmadge nevertheless soon turned his ire on the University of Georgia and the teachers' college in Statesboro, now Georgia Southern. Informants with axes to grind told Talmadge that the dean of the School of Education at the university and the Statesboro president favored school integration. The dean, Talmadge wrote, "was reared in Iowa where white and colored are taught in the same classrooms."

The Talmadge-dominated board of regents obliged the governor's tirade by firing the two main offenders and eight others. Close advisors counseled the governor to back away from the issue, but he persisted, defending his action in a broadcast speech which exuded traditional racist paternalism: "The good Negroes . . . don't want any co-mixing of the races." On another occasion Talmadge intoned, "We in the South love the Negro in his place—but his place is at the back door." The whole flap cost the white state colleges their accreditation and probably lost the governorship for Talmadge.

Young Attorney General Ellis G. Arnall emerged as the anti-Talmadge candidate in 1942. Calling the governor a Hitler-like dictator, Arnall made academic freedom and the return of university accreditation his campaign themes. Actually, Arnall and most of the so-called "better element" who supported him remained just as firmly opposed to integration as Talmadge, but they were urbane rather than vitriolic in their racism. The young man convincingly won the election, becoming the first governor to serve under a new constitutional amendment authorizing four-year terms.

Arnall was (and still is) a resident of Newnan, yet he did (and still does) retain ties with the lawyer-banker elite of Atlanta. Businesspeople appeared delighted to be rid of Talmadge's antics and reveled in the favorable national press attention which the youthful and vigorous governor brought to the Empire State. Arnall restored accreditation, fought against freight rates discriminatory to southern shippers, and engineered the passage of a revised state constitution providing for a politically independent board of regents.

His term ended in the most bizarre episode in Georgia political history. The 1946 Democratic primary election pitted the ever-present Eugene Talmadge against a field led by James V. Carmichael of Marietta, wartime head of the Bell Bomber plant. Former Governor Rivers was also in the race. With the opposing factions split, Talmadge carried the county units even though he trailed Carmichael by about 15,000 popular votes.

Talmadge's health failed as the November general election approached, and it appeared that he might die before his inauguration. Pundits observed that only Gene Talmadge could have gotten all Georgians to pray at once—half for him and half against him. His strategists also quietly arranged for a few hundred supporters to write in Herman Talmadge's name so that the younger man would command second place;

the compliant legislature would, therefore, designate him governor if his father died.

Just before Christmas the elder Talmadge passed away and the scramble was on. The legislature chose Herman Talmadge as expected, but Governor Arnall insisted that his rightful successor should be M.E. Thompson, who had been duly elected to the newly created position of lieutenant governor.

In the wee hours of the morning on January 15, 1947, the Talmadge entourage burst into the governor's office demanding to take over. Arnall later remembered a scene akin to that of "a South American banana republic, with all the commotion and fighting and cussing and whatnot." Talmadge had the advantage of the loyalty of the state patrol and Adjutant General Marvin Griffin and his National Guard.

The next day Arnall arrived at the executive suite in the capitol to find the locks changed and Talmadge forces occupying the premises. With great flourish, Arnall converted the information counter in the rotunda into a rival governor's office. For effect Arnall also took a group of reporters to the governor's mansion for lunch, even though he had already moved out. Highway patrol troopers barred his entrance, however, and on January 18, 1947, Arnall resigned in favor of Thompson.

With the support of the attorney general, Thompson set up a downtown office and initiated legal proceedings to verify his claim. He also implied that he might even request federal troops. Talmadge made a grandstand offer to the legislature that they both resign and run in an immediate special election allowing "the white people of Georgia" to decide the matter; Thompson declined.

Confusion was rampant. The wily Secretary of State Ben Fortson withheld the Georgia seal from both men. The affair was further muddled by charges that came to light in early March. Carmichael and the token Republican candidate, whose name had not even appeared on the official ballot, may have actually received more legitimate write-in votes than Herman Talmadge. According to reports, election officials in Telfair County, the Talmadge home, had belatedly produced some 50 fraudulent votes for their favorite. The *Atlanta Journal* headlined: "Telfair Dead Were Voted." The national press delighted in another display of Georgia's rough and tumble politics.

After two months of Talmadge rule, the Georgia

This sign, once visible on Savannah's West Broad Street, is representative of the legal segregation that existed throughout the South. Courtesy, Georgia Department of Archives and History

Supreme Court finally declared that the legislature had exceeded its authority; Thompson was the rightful governor. Although Thompson compiled a creditable record by championing education, improving the highway system, and purchasing Jekyll Island for the state, his days were numbered.

When Talmadge reluctantly complied with the order removing him as governor, he vowed that he would rely on "the court of last resort—the people" in the next election. The people spoke, and Talmadge defeated Thompson in a 1948 special election and again in 1950 for a full four-year term. Each time the popular vote was fairly close, but Talmadge's rural support gave him wide margins in the county unit total.

Aside from his defiant segregationist stance, Talmadge proved an effective governor—much more progressive than his father. The governor's major accomplishments included adoption of a sales tax, new highway construction, prison reform, and better public education.

Unable to succeed himself as governor after six years, Herman Talmadge turned his sights on the United States Senate. Even the venerable Senator Walter George, who had served since 1922 and had defeated Gene Talmadge in 1938, despaired facing the exceedingly popular son. The veteran senator thus gracefully retired, opening the way for Talmadge to pummel the now hapless M.E. Thompson with over 80 percent of the vote. Through his victory, Herman Talmadge joined ranks with another senator who had defeated his father—the powerful and distinguished Richard B. Russell.

Two longtime Talmadge associates followed him as governor. Lieutenant Governor Marvin Griffin moved up to the number-one spot in 1954, and Lieutenant Governor Ernest Vandiver, Jr., took the reins four years later.

As of World War II, Georgia blacks remained thoroughly segregated from white society and effectively eliminated from politics. Jim Crow laws still separated the races in public places and on public conveyances. The Democratic white primary, the poll tax, the literacy test, and old-fashioned intimidation continued to be virtually insurmountable barriers to black political participation. Twenty-five years later desegregation was the law of the land, and Georgia politics underwent fundamental transformations. To be sure, racial discrimination remained, but a generation of change brought about real progress in Georgia race relations.

The first big shift came with the elimination of the poll tax in the new state constitution of 1945 and the outlawing of all-white primaries by the United States Supreme Court the previous year. Organizations such as the Atlanta Negro Voters League immediately began registration drives, and over 100,000 blacks signed up to vote in time for the 1946 primary. Restoration of the white primary became a standard campaign promise for the Talmadge faction, although they knew that their goal could not be accomplished, given the court's ruling.

The new voters' impact appeared evident when Atlanta blacks provided the margin of victory for Helen Douglas Mankin, Georgia's first female member of the U.S. House of Representatives, who won her seat in a February 1946 special election. Eugene Talmadge expressed white supremacist sentiment, railing against "the spectacle of Atlanta Negroes sending a Congresswoman to Washington." An attorney and a veteran of the state legislature, Mankin's tenure lasted only for a few months. In the regular summer primary, she carried Fulton County by a wide enough margin to gain a popular vote victory, but she lost the DeKalb and Rockdale county unit votes, costing her the Democratic nomination and her seat.

Race baiting had been increasingly explicit in state politics since the Board of Regents controversy of 1941-1942, but the United States Supreme Court brought it to the fore with the 1954 *Brown v. Board of Education of Topeka* ruling. News of the use of federal troops to integrate a Little Rock, Arkansas, school in 1957 stirred the segregationists to the point of frenzy.

The nearly unanimous white response became known as "massive resistance." Georgia's entire congressional delegation endorsed the so-called Southern Manifesto denouncing the *Brown* decision, and the political leaders accused the high court of "destroying the amicable relations between the white and Negro races that have been created through ninety years of patient effort by the good people of both races. It has planted hatred and suspicion where there has been heretofore friendship and understanding."

The Confederate battle flag became an important symbol of Jim Crow and resistance to federal authority. In 1956 the General Assembly clearly showed defiance by redesigning the state flag. The red, white, and red bars of the lesser-known early Confederate banner were removed from the right side and replaced with the familiar battle emblem. Georgia law had long specifically prohibited blacks and whites from attending the same schools, but new statutes were passed to require the state to cut off funds to any district attempting integration. The state board of education even banned a textbook because it audaciously taught "that white people are unfair to Negroes."

Southern white politicians became masters at using the high-toned rhetoric of states' rights to obscure their racist intentions. Legislatures in Georgia and several other states revived the old, discredited doctrine of nullification, approving resolutions which declared the *Brown* decision to be "null, void, and of no force or effect."

In a classic example of massive resistance rhetoric, Congressman Jack Flynt of Griffin rose on the house floor to scathe the *Brown* decision and endorse nullification. He commenced by characterizing the United States Constitution as "the most sacred and divinely inspired instrument" since the Ten Commandments and the Sermon on the Mount. Despite the fact that he was fighting for segregation, with great solemnity he pleaded, "I am here and now willing to take a solemn oath that I hold no malice, hatred, or prejudice whatsoever in my heart, in my mind, or in my soul, against any man . . . because of his race or the color of his skin."

Marvin Griffin, during his successful 1954 gubernatorial campaign, called segregation and the county-unit system "Georgia's two greatest traditions"; his inaugural address promised "no mixing of the races" in the schools under the new administration. Ernest Vandiver, Griffin's lieutenant governor and successor, gained notoriety by pledging that "No, not one" black child would enter white schools while he served. Vandiver later would look back and regret his infamous ultimatum for two reasons: history had proven him wrong and his own attitudes on race ultimately changed. In 1961 during Vandiver's term, two blacks, Charlayne Hunter and Hamilton Holmes, entered the University of Georgia amid tense confrontation. Both have gone on to distinguished careers—Hunter as a journalist and Holmes as a physician. Later that year the Atlanta public schools began token integration without major incident.

The calm leadership of Atlanta banker John Sibley helped save Georgia from much of the ugly confrontation plaguing some other southern states. As chairman of a commission which held statewide hearings, he diffused opposition and provided a forum for those who wanted to preserve public education more than they wanted to glorify segregation.

Politics of the old order suffered a fatal blow in 1962, when a federal district court voided the county unit system. Along with legislative malapportionment, this electoral mechanism had kept rural Georgia in power by giving the smallest counties two units; a middle group, four; and the largest, six.

The 1962 Democratic primary was conducted by popular vote, and the results reflected the change. Former Governor Griffin and his openly racist campaign might have won under the old unit method, despite lingering charges of corruption during his term. Yet, the popular contest was much better suited to "cuff links" Carl Sanders. The sophisticated Augustan went on television, promising a "New Georgia" of political moderation and economic progress. The rural vote proved close, but Sanders won by running up impressive metropolitan margins, especially in black and affluent white precincts.

Court-mandated reapportionment also changed the composition of the General Assembly beginning in the 1963 session. Litigation continued for several years, but by the mid-1960s both Georgia houses finally reflected the "one person, one vote" principle. The delegations from metropolitan areas, especially Atlanta, increased substantially. Fulton County, for example, went from a single senator to seven, one of whom, Leroy Johnson, was black. For the first time in the twentieth century, Negro faces graced the General Assembly.

Tokenism still characterized much of the racial change, however, and Georgia substantially remained a Jim Crow state as late as 1964. Only a tiny fraction of the public schools were integrated; a miniscule number of blacks held public office. Restaurants and hotels continued to refuse service, while employers persisted in discrimination. But by the end of the decade the legal foundation of Jim Crow had crumbled; most of its visible manifestations fell with it.

The Civil Rights Act of 1964 outlawed employment discrimination and segregation in restaurants, hotels, and other public places. Then came the Voting

Rights Act of 1965 which provided significant federal enforcement and greatly increased black voter registration. Open housing became law in 1968.

White Georgia reacted to these changes in different ways. The larger cities, especially Atlanta, responded most positively. (The Atlanta story can be found in Chapter Ten.) Many rural areas and small towns, however, refused substantive change. The schools remained effectively separate because most white children were sent to private, often church-related, "segregation academies." Job discrimination reigned rampant and black property ownership remained limited. Electoral systems—especially the choice of at-large county commissioners, city council members, and school board officials—often kept blacks from attaining leadership positions.

Augusta provides an example of how a small metropolis made gradual steps toward integration, thanks to federal court orders, local black activism, and white business concern for order and stability. Even before the *Brown* decision, the city had hired black policemen and elected a black administrator from Paine College to the school board. Yet in 1954, Augusta became the home of the white Citizens Council movement, loosely led by Talmadge ally and virulent segregationist Roy Harris. In contrast to Harris, Mayor Millard Beckum gradually acknowledged the need for change. Black students were arrested for trying to ride in the front of a bus and a scuffle broke out at a lunch counter during a sit-in at the end of 1960. Within two years, however, both the buses and luncheonettes were integrated; blacks had exerted pressure on white business leaders who feared that confrontation—along with bad national publicity—would hamper their industrial recruitment efforts and potentially mar the city's showcase event, the Masters Golf Tournament.

Regrettably, bad publicity came anyway. Two white youths were killed following three days of rock throwing and scuffling which erupted as blacks demonstrated for jobs at a market chain. Some feared that Augusta was on the verge of a major riot, but calm prevailed.

Augustans boastful of their accomplishments received a real shock in 1970 when the beating death of a black prisoner touched off another race riot. Fires blazed, some whites were beaten, and police shot six black suspected looters. National Guard troops had to be called in to maintain order.

Above: *The grave of the Reverend Martin Luther King, Jr., Nobel Peace Prize recipient and Civil Rights leader, rests in the courtyard of the Martin Luther King Center for Nonviolent Social Change in Atlanta. The King Center sponsors social welfare activities and contains a small museum honoring the Civil Rights movement and King's career. Courtesy, The Martin Luther King Center for Nonviolent Social Change, Inc.*

Right: *Martin Luther King, Jr. Courtesy, The Martin Luther King, Jr., Center for Nonviolent Social Change, Inc.*

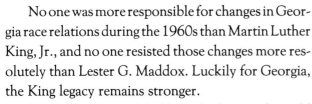

No one was more responsible for changes in Georgia race relations during the 1960s than Martin Luther King, Jr., and no one resisted those changes more resolutely than Lester G. Maddox. Luckily for Georgia, the King legacy remains stronger.

Nothing in Lester Maddox's background would lead one to believe that he might become governor. Born and reared in a working-class area of Atlanta near the Atlantic Steel plant where his father worked, Maddox held several different jobs in the late 1930s and during World War II. He finally settled into the restaurant business in 1947; his cafeteria-style Pickrick near Georgia Tech became famous for fried chicken.

What brought Maddox into the public eye were his weekly "Pickrick Says" newspaper advertisements which started in 1949. After the *Brown* decision, the homespun adages became explicitly political, often vigorously assailing integration. In 1957 and again in 1961, Maddox ran for mayor against William B. Hartsfield and Ivan Allen, Jr., respectively. Each time he carried the working-class and lower-middle-class white vote, only to be defeated by a coalition of blacks and affluent whites. Maddox urged the electorate not to be influenced by the "race-mixing liberals" of the *Atlanta Journal* and *Constitution* newspapers. With his

strong showing among white voters, Maddox decided to try the 1962 statewide race for lieutenant governor; he lost in the runoff.

The erstwhile restaurateur had failed to ride the race issue into city hall or the state capitol, but the events of 1964 began the process which would transform a three-time loser into Georgia's chief executive. The Civil Rights Act of 1964 required the desegregation of restaurants, but Maddox defiantly refused to serve blacks at the Pickrick. A series of pistol-brandishing, pick-handle-waving confrontations made Maddox a folk hero with many white Georgians. One of his "Pickrick Says" ads clarified his position: "Just in case some of you Communists, Socialists, and other Integrationists have any doubt—THE PICKRICK WILL NEVER BE INTEGRATED."

Capitalizing on his notoriety, Maddox decided to run for governor. Most political observers discounted his chances against a strong Democratic field that included Albany publisher James Gray, State Senator Jimmy Carter, and former Governor Ellis Arnall. But the feisty Maddox confounded the experts by defeating Arnall in a runoff to win the nomination. Maddox's campaign rhetoric may be best captured by a preposterous assertion that Ellis Arnall was "a wild

Socialist who is the granddaddy of forced racial integration."

What followed in the next few months proved unusual even for a state known for colorful episodes. Not since the three-governor controversy of 1946-1947 had there been such confusion, and Ellis Arnall once again found himself in the middle of it all. West Georgia Congressman Howard "Bo" Callaway, who had just won his seat in 1964, was the Republican nominee. Much of the better element voted for him that November, and he actually outpolled Maddox. Enough blacks and white liberals, however, had written in Arnall's name that the congressman did not possess a legal majority of votes. The state constitution provided for the General Assembly to choose the governor in such a case. Knowing that the heavily Democratic body would select Maddox, the ACLU and others asked the courts to order a runoff election. But the state and federal supreme courts upheld the law, and in January 1967 Maddox was chosen.

Maddox's policies proved surprisingly progressive, especially in the area of financial support for education. He boldly called for a much needed tax increase to improve state services, but the legislature turned him down. Maddox even appointed a few blacks to state boards. His speeches, however, continued to include strident attacks on integrationists, hippies, liberals, and, most of all, communists.

Enough white Georgians liked the sound of Lester Maddox so that when he was unable to succeed himself as governor, they overwhelmingly elected him lieutenant governor in 1970. By 1974, however, the Pickrick magic had worn thin, and in his bid to return to the top spot, Maddox lost to George Busbee.

Standing in stark contrast to the former restaurateur was another native Atlantan, Martin Luther King, Jr. Son of a prominent local minister, King entered Morehouse College at age 15 and then went north to Crozer Seminary and Boston University for theological study. His first pastorate was in Montgomery, Alabama, where he came to prominence as a leader of the famous 1955 bus boycott. Two years later, 60 black ministers joined King in forming the Southern Christian Leadership Conference.

Already dedicated to Mahatma Ghandi's nonviolent moral suasion methods, he further developed his philosophy with a trip to India in 1959. The following year King moved back to Atlanta, serving with his father as co-pastor of Ebenezer Baptist Church and devoting most of his time to civil rights work.

His eloquence and his persistence attracted national and worldwide attention, and he received many honors, including an audience with Pope Paul VI. To millions of Americans, the high point of King's career was his stirring "I Have a Dream" speech from the steps of the Lincoln Memorial. In January 1964 *Time* magazine designated King its "Man of the Year," and in December he was awarded the Nobel Peace Prize. With the prodding of Mayor Ivan Allen, Jr., Atlanta's business community hosted a large interracial banquet to honor King for this much esteemed, global citation.

White critics regarded King as a rabble rouser, and some, including Lester Maddox, even accused him of being a communist. On orders from J. Edgar Hoover, the Federal Bureau of Investigation kept him under constant surveillance. Some black critics, nevertheless, thought that King's nonviolence was too timid.

The next four years involved the leader in marches and demonstrations for voting rights and poor people's needs. He also became an outspoken critic of American involvement in the Vietnam War. On the evening of April 4, 1968, King was struck down by an assassin's bullet as he stood on the balcony of a Memphis motel room. The news of his death touched off rioting in many cities, but Atlanta remained calm. Mayor Allen, with the quiet approval of Coca-Cola's Robert Woodruff, arranged public support and protection for the funeral march. Governor Maddox, meanwhile, cowered in the capitol behind a cordon of state troopers.

Martin Luther King, Jr.'s, legacy lives throughout the nation, but it is especially evident in Georgia and Atlanta. His widow, Coretta Scott King, directs the Martin Luther King Center for Nonviolent Social Change. Some of his civil rights partners, including Atlanta Mayor Andrew Young and Congressman John Lewis, have achieved Southern political prominence.

Martin Luther King, Jr., lived to see most of his movement's *legal* goals accomplished. The dream of little children of both races learning and playing together also had been at least partially realized, yet *de facto* segregation and the goal of affirmative action remained. However, thanks to King and tens of thousands of others—black and white—who shared his vision, the Empire State and the South were on the verge of a new era.

# 10

## A TALE OF

## TWO GEORGIAS

*President Jimmy Carter returned to visit his home in Plains, Georgia, during his term in office. Courtesy, Jimmy Carter Library*

*Early morning snow blankets Marietta Square, lending a quiet, timeless quality to this town, the seat of Cobb County, located just 17 miles northwest of Atlanta. Photo by Arni Katz*

If in 1866, or even 1966, a scholarly university study had declared that there were "two Georgias," it certainly would have meant two separate and distinctly unequal societies—one white, one black. Yet when University of Georgia professor Charles F. Floyd released just such a report in 1986, the two Georgias of which he spoke were not black Georgia and white Georgia, but rather two separate economic states. One was a urban network with a flourishing capital city area, and the other, a conglomeration of sluggish small towns and troubled farms. Rural Georgia's economy depended heavily on agriculture and textile manufacturing—and both appeared to be in deep trouble in the mid-1980s. Non-metropolitan Georgia lost 8,000 factory jobs, mostly in textiles and apparel, from 1980 to 1986. During the same period, south Georgia farmland values dropped by a third or more, and the acreage in row crops declined by 35 percent.

Governor Joe Frank Harris tried to downplay the two-Georgia concept for fear that it would hamper industrial recruitment efforts, but the statistical evidence remained compelling. "The two Georgias is obvious on the face of it," opined economic forecaster Donald Ratajczak, "whatever the governor says."

Historically, however, the impressive story does not revolve around the sectors of the Empire State which remain impoverished and backward, but around those which have thoroughly entered the national economic mainstream after generations of lagging far behind the North and West. Indeed, since 1950, Georgia has grown faster than any other southeastern state except Florida. At the time of the stock market crash of 1929, Georgia's per capita personal income was only about half the national average. The figure approached 60 percent as World War II ended. By 1964, 70 percent had been reached, and 20 years later the state attained almost 90 percent of the national average.

The principal ingredient in Georgia's economic advance is Atlanta, a booming Sunbelt metropolis that finally began to match its boosters' dreams. Despite the state's impressive gains in personal income, only five counties, all in metropolitan Atlanta, actually exceeded the national average. Eight more reached 90 percent of the national figure, and four of them were in metro Atlanta also. In contrast, 75 of Georgia's 159 counties had per

*An isolated barn stands dusted by a fall of Christmas morning snow outside of Clayton, in Rabun County, at the extreme northeast tip of the state. Sparsely populated, the Blue Ridge Province of Georgia receives the heaviest precipitation in the state—an average of 75 inches anually. Photo by Ami Katz*

capita personal incomes of less than 70 percent of the national average. According to Neal Peirce, author of several works on American states, Atlanta's rise is the reason that the old nickname, Empire State of the South, "fits better than ever."

The capital city became Georgia's largest shortly after the Civil War. But as late as the eve of World War II, the gap between Atlanta and the state's four other large cities seemed modest compared to what it would be only four decades later. In 1940 the *combined* metropolitan populations of Augusta, Columbus, Macon, and Savannah nearly matched the Atlanta metro (471,242 to 518,100). The smaller cities had slightly more than doubled their total by 1980, but during the same period the capital's resident count nearly quadrupled. A gap of fewer than 50,000, therefore, grew into a chasm of nearly a million, and the margin has widened through the 1980s.

Though not as marked, a similar trend occurred within the region. Atlanta already served as an important southern urban center by World War II, but it could not yet lay full claim to being Dixie's premier metropolis. New Orleans was larger, and Memphis and Birmingham remained only slightly smaller. The Alabama steel city trailed Atlanta by a scant 35,000 in 1940, but only 20 years later the difference had ballooned to 400,000.

According to official estimates, the population of greater Atlanta reached one million in October 1959. The Chamber of Commerce marked the milestone with a special day of celebration. National journalists noted the occasion with words that would have been music to Henry Grady's ears. "The Georgia capital," *Newsweek* proclaimed, "is the nerve center of the New South." Meanwhile, the 1960 census revealed that neither New Orleans nor Memphis nor Birmingham had yet reached the magic million.

A major key to the postwar growth, in the words of former governor Ellis Arnall, was Atlanta's newly acquired status as "the financial and wholesale and transportation capital of the South." The old "Gate City" nickname had never been more apt. Certainly manufacturing remained important (providing 53,000 jobs and engaging 19 percent of the workforce in 1950), but the trade and service sectors stood at the heart of Atlanta's diversified economy.

Despite the abandonment of several hundred miles of track and the virtual end of passenger service since World War II, railroads have continued to be crucial to Georgia and its capital. The efforts of Governor Arnall and the Georgia Freight Bureau successfully eliminated the rate differentials which hampered southern development through the war years.

A major railroad connection from its very inception, Atlanta has also developed into a significant trucking center. Farsighted planning led the Gate City to build its early expressways in anticipation of the federal interstate highway system. Three major routes (I-20, I-75, and I-85) came together downtown, and 1970 marked the completion of the 64-mile I-285 which drew a circle around the city about nine miles from its center. This highway became a magnet for development, especially along the northern crescent.

Superior highway connections yielded more than 70 major truck terminals and over 300 Atlanta-based trucking companies by 1980. "The big industries, the big manufacturers," remarked a transportation executive, "think of Atlanta as one big warehouse."

For the Gate City to obtain regional leadership in transportation, railroads and highways was not enough. Air transport appeared to be the key to future development, and no one was more aware of that than longtime Atlanta Mayor William Hartsfield. Beginning in the 1920s as an alderman, he worked tirelessly to convince the city to obtain, then upgrade, the airport on the south edge of town. In 1941, with only 400 employees, Delta Airlines moved its headquarters from Monroe, Louisiana, to the Atlanta airport. A gleaming new high rise terminal opened just as Hartsfield left office in 1961, and the airport today bears his name. He would no doubt be proud that recent studies have declared the newest terminal, opened in 1980, to be the best-liked and first- or second-busiest airport in the country. Nonstop service now connects Atlanta with about 135 United States cities and a dozen foreign ones. Proximity to Hartsfield International is often cited as a central factor for businesses deciding to locate or expand in the Atlanta area.

The Port of Savannah now ranks twelfth in the nation in import-export dollar volume, recently surpassing Charleston and Jacksonville to become the

Facing page: *The steam locomotive* Texas *was restored in the mid-1950s for the purpose of re-creating its historic role in the Andrews Raid of the Civic War. This re-creation was to be used in the movie* The Great Locomotive Chase. *Courtesy, Georgia Department of Archives and History*

Below: *The 1948 Atlanta Municipal Airport was a prototype for the young airline industry. Courtesy, Atlanta Historical Society*

largest shipping center between Norfolk and New Orleans. Kaolin clay, used for paper and porcelain manufacture, is its number one commodity, and in fact, Georgia produces about 80 percent of the nation's supply. In containerized cargo, Savannah even exceeds Houston and New Orleans. "From a pure economic perspective," noted the president of the Savannah Port Authority, "Atlanta may benefit at least equally to Savannah because the goods that come in here can be in Atlanta the next day."

Although Atlanta now plays host to a number of national corporate headquarters—including those of Coca-Cola, BellSouth, Georgia Pacific, Southern Company, Continental Telecom, Gold Kist, and, most recently, RJR-Nabisco—it was the city's role in providing regional offices for many companies, including IBM and AT&T, that actually accounted for much of its growth. Several federal government agencies also have their regional headquarters there. Atlanta also houses the southern bureaus of most national wire services and magazines. Ted Turner's "Super Station" and his Cable News Network deliver their broadcasts from this thriving metropolis.

John Portman's development in 1960 of the oft-

expanded, 22-story, downtown merchandise mart solidified Atlanta's position as the principal regional distribution center. From this enterprise grew the Peachtree Center complex, which would dominate the central business district. The much-imitated, Portman-built Hyatt Regency with its open atrium sparked a hotel-building boom that lasted 20 years. Along with the city's civic center and the state-owned Georgia World Congress Center, travel industry expansion put Atlanta in the top ten of the country's convention cities. The city was chosen to host the 1988 Democratic National Convention.

Several institutions of higher learning also brought national attention to Atlanta. Long a respected training center for engineers, the Georgia Institute of Technology has significantly increased its research and development role. In the heart of downtown, Georgia State University enrolls over 20,000. On the northeast side of town, Emory University, heavily endowed with Coca-Cola money, steadily built its reputation, especially in medicine. The predominantly black Atlanta University Center (including Morehouse, Spelman, Clark, and Morris Brown colleges, Atlanta University, and Interdenominational Theological Seminary) on the west side preserved Atlanta's reputation as a mecca of black education. By the 1970s, thousands of black students also attended other area colleges, particularly Georgia State and Atlanta Junior College.

No southern city had a major league baseball team in the 1960s, and Atlanta boosters desperately wanted one. Mayor Allen believed that if the city built a big-league stadium, big-league sports would follow. With the financial endorsement of Mills Lane, Jr., of C & S Bank, Allen and the stadium authority decided to locate the facility on an urban renewal site adjacent to the giant interstate highway interchange just south of the capitol. In the spring of 1965, a scant 51 weeks after ground breaking, the $18-million project was complete. Braves baseball moved in from Milwaukee a year later, and that fall the Falcons began play as a National Football League expansion team. In 1968 the Hawks of the National Basketball League arrived from St. Louis, giving Atlanta big-league franchises in all three major sports. The prestige and economic impact of being the South's first major-league city proved enormous. All eyes of the sports world focused on Atlanta stadium in 1974 when Hank Aaron broke Babe Ruth's home run record.

One important factor (but difficult to quantify) in Atlanta's economic resurgence was its reputation as a city of racial moderation during the turbulent 1950s and 1960s. Business and political leaders carefully cultivated an exaggerated, though not entirely undeserved, image of Atlanta as the city "too busy to hate."

An uneasy coalition of black and affluent white voters kept moderate whites such as mayors Hartsfield and Allen in office. The black electorate was nurtured by ministers, professors, and other black professionals, including Clarence Bacote, Grace Hamilton, and A.T. Walden. Arch-segregationist Lester Maddox ran for mayor against Hartsfield in 1957 and against Allen four years later. Each time the black and affluent white coalition prevailed.

Atlanta business basked in this reputation for moderation. As early as 1957 *Time Magazine* called the city an "oasis of tolerance." The "too busy to hate" phrase, first quoted nationally in the October 19, 1959, *Newsweek,* seemed to be validated by the city's smooth handling of the court-ordered desegregation of four all-white high schools in Sep-

tember 1961.

Meanwhile, business and political leaders led by Chamber of Commerce President Ivan Allen negotiated with student protestors, Martin Luther King, Jr., and the older black establishment to arrange for voluntary desegregation of most downtown business establishments. This occurred three years before federal law required it. Later, as mayor, Allen was the only prominent white politician from the South to testify before Congress in favor of the Civil Rights Act of 1964. The city escaped major race riots during the tense 1965-1968 years, although one minor outbreak took place on the southside.

Most of the metropolitan population growth after World War II occurred outside the Atlanta city limits, so the municipality became increasingly black. The city claimed 68,000 fewer whites and 162,000 more blacks in 1980 than 30 years earlier. With this demographic shift came political power for urban blacks. No longer would they content themselves with being the swing vote between white factions; they could control. The turning point came when former King aide Andrew Young went to Congress in 1972 and black attorney Maynard Jackson became Atlanta's mayor the following year. Young succeeded Jackson in 1981 and easily won reelection four years later. In another landmark, two black men, Atlanta Life Insurance Company President Jesse Hill and contractor Herman Russell, served as presidents of the Atlanta Chamber of Commerce.

Transportation, vigorous boosterism, and racial harmony continue to attract jobs to Atlanta. In the early 1980s the Atlanta Chamber of Commerce cooperated with suburban chambers to form the Metropolitan Atlanta Committee for Economic Development (MACFED) and to launch a multimillion dollar promotion effort. This effort at least partially resulted in gains comparable to those made by the "Forward Atlanta" campaigns of the 1920s and 1960s. By 1986 metropolitan Atlanta contained nearly half of all the nonagricultural jobs in Georgia.

As early as 1958 *Reader's Digest* credited Atlanta with "the best race relations of any city in the deep south." After some dozen years of tough but steady change, Benjamin E. Mays, the black president of Morehouse College and the Atlanta

A loaded logging truck stands ready to transport its snow-covered cargo in north Georgia. The state's Blue Ridge Province, which also contains Georgia's highest peak, Brasstown Bald (4,784 feet), is sparsely populated, and has thick stands of pine and hardwoods. Photo by Arni Katz

School Board, could state in his autobiography, "Atlanta is not the typical South. It is better." Mayor Maynard Jackson was willing to take the city's comparison beyond Dixie despite his occasional difficulties with the white business community and others. "Atlanta," he boasted in 1981, "has the best race relations of any city in the country." Of course, everything was far from perfect. Tensions remained and discrimination persisted.

Racial harmony, new development, and better transportation tell only part of the story, however. Much of the economic growth in both Georgias, but especially in the metropolitan areas, can be attributed to the massive influx of defense-related dollars. World War II and the Korean War started an industrial buildup which continued through the Cold War era. At the height of the Vietnam War, over 100,000 servicemen and women were stationed in the state. Almost half that many civilians worked at the bases and posts, and another 40,000 flocked to military-related contractors. The Defense Department now lists 23 installations in Georgia. Fort Benning at Columbus, Fort Gordon at Augusta, Fort Stewart and Hunter Army Air Field near Savannah, and Robins Air Force Base south

of Macon are the largest. Other major facilities include Dobbins Air Force Base, Marietta Naval Air Station, Fort McPherson, and Fort Gillem in metro Atlanta; Moody Air Force Base in Valdosta; Marine Corps Logistic Base in Albany; Naval Supply Corps School in Athens; and Kings Bay Submarine Base in St. Mary's.

With the retirement of Representative Carl Vinson in 1965 and the death of Senator Richard B. Russell six years later, Georgia lost the unique clout that came with the chairmanships of the armed services committees in both houses of Congress. In January 1987, however, a Georgian once again headed the Senate Armed Services Committee, as Senator Sam Nunn assumed the influential post.

The impact of defense dollars on the state has been enormous, and all indications point to continuing prosperity in that sector. Since the bulk of the activity remains outside of metropolitan Atlanta, defense expenditures help keep the distinction between the two Georgias from being even more marked than it is. In all, the state's Department of Defense installations employed over 120,000 military and civilian personnel with an annual payroll

exceeding $2.2 billion in 1984, ranking Georgia fifth in the nation. Considering contracts as well as bases and posts, the military poured approximately $9 billion into the state's economy in 1985.

Georgia politics also has seen changes. No openly segregationist, race-baiting candidates have won statewide office in twenty years. Instead of vying with each other over their dedication to the "southern way of life," most politicians of the 1970s and 1980s at least give lip service to racial brotherhood. The modern candidates concentrate on governmental economy, educational improvement, and industrial development.

This political watershed is personified by Jimmy Carter. His 1970 campaign for governor reeked with old-style rhetoric, but his governorship proved thoroughly modern. Carter moved quickly to put the campaign, and thus the politics of the past, behind him. The governor's inaugural address caught the attention of the nation. "I say to you quite frankly," he declared, "that the time for racial discrimination is over . . ." Without such a statement, Jimmy Carter would never have become president.

As Georgia's chief executive, Carter returned to his curious mixture of conservatism, liberalism, populism, and religion, which historian Gary Fink called "temperamental pragmatism." Carter retained some of the technician's approach that he had learned as an Annapolis graduate and nuclear submarine officer.

Carter's four years in office were marked by awkward relations with the legislative body—a problem which would also plague his White House years. The governor quickly split with Lester Maddox, a constant irritant from his new position as lieutenant governor and presiding officer of the state Senate. Still, Carter boasted accomplishments. The hallmark of his administration was a major reorganization of the executive branch. Strides in race relations included the appointment of blacks to the board of regents and about fifty other positions on commissions. For the first time, portraits of blacks graced the capitol building as Carter hung paintings of Martin Luther King, Jr., and two other blacks.

The transformation from "Jimmy Who," the progressive southern governor, to James Earl Carter, president from Georgia, is a story that cannot be told here. Still, the Carter presidency proved undeniably good for the state. The national

press focused on things Georgian and almost fawned over Miss Lillian, Carter's Peace Corps-volunteer mother. Journalists sometimes appeared inhospitable to Carter and his gaggle of Georgians (especially brother Billy), but their jibes usually lacked the acerbic tone previously directed at the white supremacist politicians—Talmadge, Griffin, and Maddox—of the old era. When Americans elected as president the first true sitting son of the Deep South since the Civil War, they permanently altered the face of national politics.

In more regional terms, the last four decades have witnessed rising black influence and the increasing popularity of the Republican party. Though not immune to either force, Georgia state government nevertheless remains firmly in white Democratic hands. Republicans have carried Georgia at the presidential level since 1964, except when Jimmy Carter and George Wallace carried the vote. Two of Georgia's ten congressional seats have gone to Republicans, and in 1980 Mack Mattingly became the first GOP candidate of the twentieth century to be elected to the U.S. Senate, though Atlanta Democrat Wyche Fowler defeated him six years later. State GOP leaders were encouraged by

Bo Callaway's showing in the unusual 1966 race against Lester Maddox, but they have not mounted a serious challenge for governor since. The Georgia General Assembly of 1952 counted no Republicans, and as late as 1962 merely two served in the house and two in the Senate. Increases notwithstanding, the GOP still has averaged only about 30 of the 236 combined seats. A loyal black following compensates for some of the suburban votes which the Democrats lost in previous decades. Black voters, for example, provided the margin of victory in Fowler's defeat of Mattingly.

Black officeholding, however, remains very limited. The year 1962 saw blacks entering the legislature for the first time in the twentieth century. Today, about 30 blacks serve. Still, those blacks who win office almost always come from black majority constituencies. Mayor Andrew Young and Congressman John Lewis, both from Atlanta, and former Augusta Mayor Edward McIntyre are prominent examples. Of Georgia's more than 7,000 elective offices, blacks held only about 250 in 1982.

Two governors succeeded Carter who prided themselves on being businesslike and respectable—some would say dull. Calling himself "a workhorse,

not a showhorse," Albany attorney and veteran state legislator George Busbee defeated Lester Maddox and Carter ally Bert Lance to win the 1974 Democratic nomination. He then trounced flamboyant Republican Ronnie Thompson in the general election.

Stagflation (simultaneous recession and inflation) dominated Busbee's first term and necessitated budget cutbacks, but the governor managed the crisis well enough to be overwhelmingly reelected. In fact, his popularity was the catalyst for the 1976 constitutional amendment allowing governors a second term.

A north Georgia Methodist followed the two southwest Georgia Baptists. Like his immediate predecessors, longtime legislator Joe Frank Harris was a small-town sophisticate from the civic club/business establishment. He also shared the political strategies advanced by Carter and Busbee: rather than attacking integration and assailing Atlanta, Harris courted the black vote and realized that the capital city was the key to Georgia prosperity. Above all, however, governors Busbee and Harris have focused on education.

Four extensive postwar studies have resulted in major legislative initiatives regarding education. The first led to the Minimum Foundation Program of 1949. This program was given a good start by Herman Talmadge's 1951 sales tax, but it never received full funding. During the administration of Carl Sanders, a second blue ribbon commission issued an extensive report which stated, "We do not think it unreasonable for the Empire State of the South to aspire to equal or exceed the national average [in teacher salaries] within a reasonable number of years." The study inspired the new and improved Minimum Foundation Program of 1964, but like its predecessor, it fell short of its goals because of inadequate financing.

Both Minimum Foundation programs floundered partly because of racial attitudes. As late as the Maddox term, almost all the state's public schools remained effectively segregated, so the taxpayers faced the task of maintaining an expensive and archaic dual system. Federal court orders and the threat of losing governmental funds finally accomplished integration by the early 1970s. Yet, in some areas, so many white students had fled the public schools that local property owners were disinclined to support ad valorem taxes above min-

Left: *President Jimmy Carter, the only U.S. president to call Georgia his home, served for one term. Courtesy, Jimmy Carter Library*

Below: *President Jimmy Carter is pictured here walking with Rosalyn Carter from the Capitol to the White House after his inauguration in 1977. Courtesy, Jimmy Carter Library*

imum levels. Furthermore, the tax base in many communities often heavily relied on declining farms; adequate funding would have been difficult even if the taxpayers had been willing. Atlanta's city schools became overwhelmingly black, while most of the surrounding systems remained predominantly white.

Aware of the continuing problems and attuned to the need to deal with the challenge of integration, the legislature authorized another major study during the Carter term. No longer satisfied with such a modest word as "minimum," but still reflecting caution, the new byword was "adequate." The Adequate Program for Education in Georgia (APEG) passed in 1974, yet the schools failed to make any notable regional or national gains. In fact, the three ambitious programs of 1949, 1964, and 1974 only kept Georgia about even, since most other southern states had also embarked on significant initiatives.

Legislators faced a formidable task if they were to solidify Georgia's Sunbelt status through quality education. Governor Joe Frank Harris strongly agreed. A fourth prestigious commission devised, and the legislature substantially adopted, what be-

came known as Quality Basic Education (QBE). Even with Governor Harris' adamant "no new taxes" pledge, economic growth yielded enough money to fund impressive teacher raises in 1985 and 1986, moving Georgia nearly to the top of the region. The national average seemed a reachable goal and test scores appeared to be on the rise.

Although skeptics remember the failed educational reforms of the past, current trends may indicate that history does not necessarily repeat itself. Optimists hope for a new day in Georgia learning and look forward to the time when the two Georgias mesh into one entity that truly deserves the name Empire State of the South.

Above: White Hall Tavern sold refreshments to thirsty travelers and local residents. Later, when the railroad chose to locate a major new line close by, the tavern's patrons saw the beginnings of the city that became Atlanta. Painting by Wilbur Kurtz. Courtesy, Franklin Garrett

Right: Where Hardy Ivy's cabin and farm once stood, the towers of downtown Atlanta now rise skyward. Painting by Wilbur Kurtz. Courtesy, Franklin Garrett

Above: *Leaders of the "New South" used expositions to promote the business of the region in the eyes of the world. These fairs were also used to entertain and educate visitors. Visitors to Atlanta's Cotton States and International Exhibition in 1895 could see a re-creation of an Eskimo village or a Cairo street, visit buildings enshrining the accomplishments of women or blacks, see exhibits of art or industrial products, and then top it off with a ride on a Ferris wheel. Courtesy, Atlanta Historical Society*

Right: *This engraving commemorated the centennial of U.S. independence and Savannah's revolutionary history. Courtesy, University of Georgia Libraries Special Collections*

An Atlanta product, Coca-Cola became a nationally recognized favorite. Courtesy, Coca-Cola Company

The 1908 road race in Savannah, sponsored by the Automobile Club of America, demonstrated Georgia's early interest in this new form of transportation. Courtesy, University of Georgia Libraries Special Collections

Right: *Kennesaw Mountain National Park was the location of the last Civil War battle before General William T. Sherman and the Union Army took Atlanta. Photo by Arni Katz*

Above: *This statue of a Confederate soldier represents the Confederate States of America. Photo by Arni Katz*

Left: *The Henry W. Grady is one of the paddlewheelers operating in the lake at Stone Mountain Park. Photo by Arni Katz*

Left: *A quiet afternoon spent under the shade of a live oak tree in Clayton, Georgia, was captured in this photo by Arni Katz.*

Facing page, top left: *This horse posed for a portrait on a farm in northern Georgia. Photo by Darline Katz*

Facing page, bottom: *This colorful autumn scene was photographed in Clayton, Georgia. Photo by Arni Katz*

Left and far left: *The dogwood tree, with its beautiful white and pink blossoms, is indigenous to Georgia. Courtesy, Atlanta Historical Society*

Above: *This roadside stand in Dahlonega is one of the many such establishments that can be found throughout the state of Georgia. Photo by Arni Katz*

Right: *This woman and her wooden menagerie participated in the Atlanta Craft Show. Photo by Arni Katz*

Above: *This Ferris wheel was part of the carnival at the Georgia State Fair. Photo by Arni Katz*

Top: *A day at the beach near St. Simon Island is sure to be a shell-collecting adventure. Photo by Arni Katz*

Left: *These two children are enjoying a day at the Atlanta Zoo. Photo by Arni Katz*

Above: *The last few leaves of this Georgia red maple tree cling to its branches as winter arrives. Photo by Arni Katz*

Left: *The weather-beaten hardwood siding of this old house in northern Georgia has stood the test of time. Photo by Arni Katz*

Top, left: *Georgia averages only five days of snowfall annually. This blanket of snow was photographed in 1983 by Arni Katz.*

Top, right: *Dogwood trees, native to Georgia, bloom between mid- and late April. They are one of the earliest indications that spring has arrived. Photo by Arni Katz*

Bottom: *Spraying a Georgia peanut crop creates a vivid rainbow of color. Photo by Arni Katz*

Below: *Sorghum, one of several native Georgia crops, is used in the production of molasses. Photo by Arni Katz*

Below: *Beets piled in a tomato box are ready for sale. Photo by Arni Katz*

Right: *Father and son pose happily with their first catch of the day. Photo by Arni Katz*

Facing page: *This peaceful spot along the Chattahoochee River has given fishermen catfish, trout, and salmon. Photo by Arni Katz*

Bottom: *Kayaking is one of the many activities available along the Chattahoochee River. Photo by Arni Katz*

Below: *This mallard drake relaxes on a log in the lake at Stone Mountain Park. Photo by Arni Katz*

Above: *The cylindrical building in this view of downtown Atlanta is the famous Peachtree Plaza Hotel, the world's tallest hotel. Photo by Arni Katz*

Right: *Many new houses are being constructed in northern Atlanta suburbs. Photo by Arni Katz*

Above: This brand-new S-shaped office building is located on Powers Ferry Road in the northwest section of Atlanta. Photo by Arni Katz

Left: Modern Atlanta policy gives the "green light" to growth and prosperity. Photo by Arni Katz

# 11

---

# EPILOGUE

---

In 1987 we ended the first edition of this book looking forward "to the time when the two Georgias mesh into one entity that truly deserves the name Empire State of the South." That day has not yet arrived, but trend lines in the three key areas of economic growth, educational improvement, and racial harmony continue to engender optimism as Georgia prepares to enter the twenty-first century.

In terms of economic growth, the most dramatic and symbolic development of the past eight years was the announcement that Atlanta and Georgia would host the 1996 Olympic Games. Atlanta won the games the way it has won so many other prizes that have made it the premier city of the South -- hard work and boosterism. Led by a determined Billy Payne and legitimized in the world's eyes by Andrew Young, Jimmy Carter, and Coca Cola, Georgia's Olympic promoters would not be discouraged even in the face of competition from sentimental favorite Athens, Greece. And they succeeded. For at least twenty-five years, Atlanta business leaders had been touting their home town as the world's next great international city -- few people took them seriously then, but now the dreams have been realized.

An economic impact study prepared as part of the Olympic bid process concluded that the positive boost would be enormous, and indeed it has been. Olympic-related construction helped pull the state's economy out of mild recession and has helped keep Georgia's growth rate well above the national average.

The focus of Olympic activity will be in a ring surrounding a revitalized downtown Atlanta. The existing Georgia Dome, Atlanta-Fulton County Stadium, Omni Arena, and World Congress Center conference hall have been joined by a brand new showcase stadium and an Olympic park paved in bricks personalized with the names of thousands of donors. The Olympic village, located on the campus of Georgia Tech just north of downtown, will leave a legacy of student housing and a world-class swimming and diving facility. Streets, highways, and the airport have been upgraded, and new downtown housing has been erected.

Olympic sites dot the suburbs as well. The equestrian venue is in Rockdale County; impressive cycling and tennis facilities have risen at Stone Mountain; rowers will compete at Lake Lanier; and the popular new sport of beach volleyball has a showcase at Jonesboro in Atlanta's southern crescent. Indeed, the entire state and region have benefitted from Atlanta's coup. From yachting at Savannah to soccer in Athens to softball in Columbus, the Olympics Games are truly a statewide endeavor.

Although Atlanta has led the economic growth of the state with glamour events like the Olympics, Super Bowl XXVIII, and the Democratic National Convention and with high profile companies like Coca-Cola, UPS, TBS/CNN, and Delta Air Lines, economic development has not been confined to the capital city metropolis. In addition to Atlanta, five other metropolitan statistical areas (Athens, Augusta, Macon, Savannah, and the Georgia portion of Chattanooga) met or exceeded the 1994-95 national rate of growth in buying power, with Augusta especially strong. The two remaining MSAs, Columbus and Albany, were not far behind. Revitalized river front convention-entertainment districts have been part of the growth story in Augusta, Columbus, and Savannah.

Thanks in part to the influence of Senator Sam Nunn, Georgia's economy has been mostly spared in the recent rounds of military cutbacks. In fact, the new submarine base at Kings Bay has given an important boost to the coastal region. Non-metropolitan areas with notable expansion include the mountains of north Georgia and the sea islands near Brunswick, which attract tourists and retirees.

There have been some remarkable stories of recovery from the devastating floods of 1994 in southwest Georgia towns such as Montezuma. The spirit of the residents carried them through, and the heart of the rest of the state went out to the victims. But, as a whole, rural south and central Georgia continue to lag behind the rest of the state in economic development.

So too have the poorer areas of the state lagged in educational improvement. One of the objectives of the Quality Basic Education (QBE) program was to diminish inequities in funding and narrow the disparity in achievement between the educational haves and have nots. But QBE was never fully funded, and parts of the program seemed to bring more paperwork than progress. No where has the problem of the "two Georgias" been more evident than in education. Some systems, mainly in the suburbs and some small cities such as Rome, boast test scores near or above national averages, but the scores are so dismal in poverty-stricken areas that the state's average is dragged down near the bottom of national rankings.

On a more positive note, thanks to Georgia's enormously successful state lottery, which the voters approved in 1992, public schools have received a significant infusion of funds for instructional technology in distance learning and computers. The lottery, which contributed $362 million to the state treasury in its first year, funded the HOPE Scholarship program, which has already helped thousands of students attend colleges and technical institutes. The popularity of the lottery and its attendant education expenditures helped propel Governor Zell Miller to reelection in 1994 over the strongest Republican challenge since Bo Callaway nearly won in 1966.

Miller wants to reform education from top to bottom. In addition to his scholarship program and technology initiative, the Governor has championed greatly expanded access to preschooling. At the same time, he has lent strong encouragement to a new chancellor who is determined to reinvigorate the state's University System.

Georgia's positive strides in race relation are symbolized by the rise of Robert Benham to the chief justiceship of the state Supreme Court and the appointment of Savannah native Clarence Thomas to the United States Supreme Court.

Not all symbols, however, are so positive. In 1956, as a symbol of defiance to racial integration, the General Assembly changed the state flag to include the Confederate battle flag. In his first term, as gesture of racial harmony, Governor Miller pledged to return the flag to the old design. It almost cost him his governorship. Despite the fact that the pre-1956 design was itself based on the Confederate stars and bars and that it had flown over more than 75 years of Confederate Memorial Days, many white voters passionately saw changing back as too much of a concession. Some white commentators tried to deny that racism and defiance of federal authority had inspired the 1956 modification, although no serious historian has any doubt about the mood of the legislative body at the time of the change. Disappointed but astute, Miller abandoned the issue prior to his reelection campaign.

Meanwhile, as a result of redistricting, two more black Georgians were elected to Congress, bringing the total to three of eleven. But as of late 1995 the future was clouded by a federal court decision that overturned Georgia's districts on the grounds that they had been racially gerrymandered. A special session of the General Assembly was called to redraw the districts, but it deadlocked along racial and partisan lines and went home in failure. Resolution lies in the hands of the courts.

The redistricting also moved Representative Newt Gingrich from the area south and west of Atlanta where he had consistently faced relatively close races to an overwhelmingly white and safely Republican district in the northern suburbs. With the Republican Congressional victory in 1994, Gingrich became the third Georgian, and the first in over one hundred years, to serve as Speaker of the House.

Episodes such as redistricting and the flag controversy plus statistics about persistent poverty and low educational achievement serve to remind Georgians that historical racial tensions have not completely disappeared. On the other hand, optimists can point to continued strides in politics and economics.

Few Georgians are more positive and upbeat than Maynard Jackson, a former two-term mayor of Atlanta, who was the first African-American to hold that position. "Any city that is not paying attention to race relations," Jackson recently told a Federal Reserve Bank conference, "is a city that will not succeed." Atlanta, Jackson declared, though "clearly not perfect, has the best race relations of any city in the United

States. Here it's understood that bad race relations is bad business."

A 1992 report by the Selig Center for Economic Growth at the University of Georgia confirms Jackson's observation and indicates that it should apply to the whole state, not just Atlanta. The report pointed out that African-Americans control 17 cents of each dollar of spending power and concluded, "Georgia's black consumers have strong economic muscles and are a substantial economic force throughout the state." Wise business men and women, black and white, know such statistics and act accordingly.

Thanks to the relatively strong economy, population has expanded, and mid 1990s estimates now place Georgia as the tenth most populous state in the union. The Empire State of the South can solidify its new found status in the mainstream as long as the state's political and business leadership can build on recent history and keep the trends toward economic development, educational improvement, and racial harmony moving in the right direction.

– Bradley R. Rice

*The Valdosta Concert Band posed in uniform with its instruments in 1920. Courtesy, Georgia Department of Archives and History, Vanishing Georgia Collection*

# BIBLIOGRAPHY

Abbot, William W. *The Royal Governors of Georgia.* Chapel Hill, N.C.: 1959.

Anderson, William. *The Wild Man from Sugar Creek: The Political Career of Eugene Talmadge.* Baton Rouge, La.: 1975.

*Atlanta Historical Journal.* Various issues.

Bartley, Numan V. *The Creation of Modern Georgia.* Athens: 1983.

———. *From Thurmond to Wallace: Political Tendencies in Georgia, 1948-1968.* Baltimore: 1970.

Bartley, Numan V., and Graham, Hugh Davis. *Southern Politics and the Second Reconstruction.* Baltimore: 1975.

Bass, Jack, and De Vries, Walter. *The Transformation of Southern Politics.* New York: 1977.

Bernard, Richard M., and Rice, Bradley R. *Sunbelt Cities.* Austin, Texas: 1983.

Bonner, James C. *A History of Georgia Agriculture, 1732-1860.* Athens: 1964.

Bryan, T. Conn. *Confederate Georgia.* Athens: 1953.

Carson, O.E. *The Trolley Titans: A Mobile History of Atlanta. Atlanta.* Glendale, Ca.: 1981.

Cashin, Edward J. *The Story of Augusta.* Augusta: 1980.

Chalmers, David M. *Hooded Americanism: The History of the Ku Klux Klan.* New York: 1976.

Coleman, Kenneth, et al. *A History of Georgia.* Athens: 1977. Rev. 1993.

———. *Colonial Georgia: A History.* New York: 1976.

———. *The American Revolution in Georgia.* Athens: 1958.

Coleman, Kenneth, and Gurr, Charles S., eds. *Dictionary of Georgia Biography.* 2 vols. Athens: 1983.

Conway, Alan. *The Reconstruction of Georgia.* Minneapolis: 1966.

Cook, James F. *Governors of Georgia.* Huntsville, Ala.: 1979. Rev. 1995.

Coulter, E. Merton. *Georgia: A Short History.* Chapel Hill, N.C.: 1960.

———. *College Life in the Old South.* Athens: 1951.

Crane, Verner W. *The Southern Frontier, 1670-1732.* Durham, N.C.: 1928.

Davis, Harold. *The Fledgling Province: A Social and Cultural History of Colonial Georgia.* Chapel Hill, N.C.: 1976.

DeBolt, Margaret Wayt. *Savannah: A Historical Portrait.* Norfolk, Va.: 1976.

Dittmer, John. *Black Georgia in the Progressive Era, 1900-1920.* Urbana, Ill: 1977.

Dyer, Thomas G. *The University of Georgia: A Bicentennial History.* Athens: 1985.

Fink, Gary M. *Prelude to the Presidency: The Political Character and Legislative Leadership Style of Governor Jimmy Carter.* Westport, Conn.: 1980.

Fite, Gilbert C. *Cotton Fields No More: Southern Agriculture, 1865-1980.* Lexington, Ky.: 1984.

Flynn, Charles L., Jr. *White Land, Black Labor: Caste and Class in Late Nineteenth-Century Georgia.* Baton Rouge, La.: 1983.

Garrett, Franklin M. *Atlanta and Environs.* 2 vols. Athens: 1969, orig. pub. 1954.

Garrison, Webb. *The Legacy of Atlanta: A Short History.* Atlanta: 1987.

*Georgia Historical Quarterly.* Various issues.

Glatthaar, Joseph T. *The March to the Sea and Beyond: Sherman's Troops in the Savannah and Carolina Campaigns.* New York: 1985.

Grantham, Dewey W. *Hoke Smith and the Politics of the New South.* Baton Rouge, La.: 1958.

Griffith, Louis T., and Talmadge, John E. *Georgia Journalism, 1763-1950.* Athens: 1951.

Grimes, Millard B., et al. *The Last Linotype: The Story of Georgia and Its Newspapers Since World War II.* Macon: 1985.

Hartshorn, Truman A., et al. *Atlanta: Metropolis in Georgia.* Cambridge, Mass.: 1976.

Hudson, Charles. *The Southeastern Indians.* Knoxville, Tenn.: 1976.

Ivers, Larry E. *British Drums on the Southern Frontier.* Chapel Hill, N.C.: 1974.

Jackson, Harvey H. *Lachlan McIntosh and the Politics of Revolutionary Georgia.* Athens: 1979.

Jackson, Harvey H., and Spalding, Phinizy, eds. *Forty Years of Diversity: Essays on Colonial Georgia.* Athens: 1984.

Jones, George F. *The Salzburger Saga: Religious Exiles and Other Germans Along the Savannah.* Athens: 1984.

Kyle, F. Clason. *Images: A Pictorial History of Columbus, Georgia.* Columbus: 1986.

Hodler, Thomas W., and Schtetter, Howard A. *The Atlas of Georgia.* Athens: 1986.

Jacoway, Elizabeth, and Colburn, David R., eds. *Southern Businessmen and Desegregation.* Baton Rouge, La.: 1982.

Joiner, Oscar H., et al. *A History of Public Education in Georgia, 1734-1976.* Columbia, S.C.: 1979.

Lamplugh, George R. *Politics on the Periphery: Factions and Parties in Georgia, 1783-1806.* Newark, N.J.: 1986.

McMath, Robert C., et al. *Engineering the New South: Georgia Tech, 1885-1985.* Athens: 1985.

Martin, Harold H. *William Berry Hartsfield: Mayor of Atlanta.* Athens: 1978.

———. *Georgia.* New York: 1976.

———. *Atlanta and Environs.* Vol. III. Athens: 1987.

Mellichamp, Josephine. *Senators From Georgia.* Huntsville, Ala.: 1976.

Miller, Zell. *Great Georgians.* Franklin Springs, Ga.: 1983.

Mohr, Clarence. *On the Threshold of Freedom: Masters and Slaves in Civil War Georgia.* Athens: 1986.

Montgomery, Horace. *Cracker Parties.* Baton Rouge, La.: 1950.

Nixon, Raymond B. *Henry Grady: Spokesman of the New South.* New York: 1943.

Parks, Joseph H. *Joseph E. Brown of Georgia.* Baton Rouge, La.: 1977.

Phillips, U.B. *Georgia and State Rights.* Washington, D.C.: 1902.

Preston, Howard L. *Automobile Age Atlanta.* Athens: 1979.

Range, Willard. *A Century of Georgia Agriculture, 1850-1950.* Athens: 1954.

Reitt, Barbara B., ed. *Georgia Women: A Celebration.* Atlanta: 1976.

Saye, Albert B. *A Constitutional History of Georgia.* Athens: 1970.

Shadgett, Olive Hall. *The Republican Party in Georgia from Reconstruction Through 1900.* Athens: 1964.

Shavin, Norman, and Galphin, Bruce. *Atlanta: Triumph of a People.* Atlanta: 1985.

Shaw, Barton C. *The Wool-Hat Boys: Georgia's Populist Party.* Baton Rouge, La.: 1984.

Shingleton, Royce. *Richard Peters: Champion of the New South.* Macon: 1985.

Sieg, Edward Chan. *Eden on the Marsh: An Illustrated History of Savannah.* Northridge, Ca.: 1985.

Simpson, John E. *Howell Cobb.* Chicago: 1973.

Smith, Julius Floyd. *Slavery and Rice Culture in Low Country Georgia, 1750-1860.* Knoxville, Tenn.: 1985.

Spalding, Phinizy. *Oglethorpe in America.* Chicago: 1977.

Talmadge, John E. *Rebecca Latimer Felton.* Athens: 1960.

*Vanishing Georgia.* From the Georgia Department of Archives and History. Athens: University of Georgia Press, 1982.

Walton, Hanes, Jr. *Invisible Politics: Black Political Behavior.* Albany, N.Y.: 1985.

Williford, William Bailey. *Americus Through the Years.* Atlanta: 1975.

Wood, Betty. *Slavery in Colonial Georgia.* Athens: 1984.

Woodward, C. Vann. *Tom Watson: Agrarian Rebel.* New York: 1938

# INDEX

**About The Authors**
**Bradley R. Rice** holds a Ph.D. in history from the University of Texas at Austin. From 1976 to the present he has been on the faculty of Clayton State College near Atlanta, where he is now Assistant Vice President for Academic Affairs. Specializing in urban and business history, Rice has written and edited three books and has published numerous articles in periodicals including the *Journal of Urban History* and the *Georgia Historical Quarterly*. Since 1983 Rice has been editor of *Atlanta History: A Journal of Georgia and the South*, a quarterly published by the Atlanta Historical Society. With Harvey Jackson, he authored the study guide for a best-selling history textbook. Active in many professional and civic associations, Rice is a past president of the Georgia Association of Historians and currently serves as a member of the Board of Curators of the Georgia Historical Society.

**Harvey H. Jackson** is Professor of History and Head of the Department of History at Jacksonville State University in Alabama. Formerly of Clayton State College, Jackson has written extensively on both Georgia and Alabama. With several books and more than two dozen articles to his credit, Jackson is a popular speaker on southern history. He earned his masters from the University of Alabama and his doctorate from the University of Georgia.